Is the Devil a Myth?

C. F. Wimberly

© 2023 Culturea Editions
Texte et illustration de couverture : © domaine public
Edition : Culturea (Hérault, 34)
Contact : infos@culturea.fr
Retrouvez notre catalogue sur http://culturea.fr
Imprimé en Allemagne par Books on Demand
Design typographique : Derek Murphy
Layout : Reedsy (https://reedsy.com/)
Dépôt légal : janvier 2023
Tous droits réservés pour tous pays
ISBN : 9791041942664

CONTENTS

PREFACE

It is the writer's firm conviction, in these days when the most enthusiastic "bookworm" cannot even keep up with the titles of the book output, that an earnest, sensible reason should be given for adding another to the already endless list of books. We have enough books to-day, "good, bad, indifferent," with which, if they were collected, to build another Cyclops pyramid. The sage of the Old Testament declared in his day, concerning the endless making of books; such a statement, compared with modern writing and publishing of books, sounds amusing.

Every possible subject, vagary, or ism, for which a book could be written, is overworked. Bible themes of all grades, from orthodoxy to ultra higher criticism, have flooded the land. Especially is the iconoclast in much evidence; he is free lance, and shows no quarters. Cardinal tenets of Bible faith, so long unquestioned, are being smitten with a merciless hand. Disintegration is the most obvious fact among us; nothing is too sacred for the crucible of what is termed "scholarship."

But why this book? Let us take a little survey. Over against the modern idea, that the race is endowed with all the inherent elements of goodness necessary to its regeneration, there is a correspondent belief that *evil* is only an error. When the race by social and mental evolution succeeds in eliminating all the superstitions and false dogmas, the body politic will be self-curative, like the physical body, restoring itself by means of inspiration, respiration, exercise, sleep, food, etc., once the causes of disease are eliminated from the system.

For several decades we have been approaching the doctrine which denies all Personalism—either good or bad. When we repudiate the

Bible teaching, that the source of all evil emanates from a great Personality, the Bible teaching of the Incarnation suffers in the same proportion.

The title of this book is a question, and one by no means strained, if considered from the view-point of modern thought. We have undertaken an answer. If by reason and revelation we can arrive at a satisfactory conclusion, the gain thereby cannot be overestimated. If the personality of Satan can be successfully consigned to the religious junk pile, our Bible is at once thrown into a jumble of contradictions and inconsistencies. The result will be even worse than our enemies claim for it now. One of the late recognized writers on the Old Testament says: "The Old Testament is no longer considered valuable among scholars as a sacred oracle, but it is valuable in that it is the history of a people." *If the Devil is a Myth, our Bible can be nothing better than historical chaos.*

In the preparation of these pages, we wish to acknowledge with deep gratitude the assistance of Mr. S. D. Gordon, author of "Quiet Talks"; Dr. I. M. Haldeman, author and preacher; Dr. Gross Alexander, editor, author, and preacher; Dr. W. B. Godbey, an author of great learning and extensive travel; Dr. B. Carradine, evangelist and author; Dr. H. C. Morrison, college president, editor, author, and evangelist; Prof. L. T. Townsend, and Hon. Philip Mauro.

If the reading of this book shall bring to any-struggling soul helpful information concerning our common Enemy, we shall be doubly repaid for the labour of its preparation. We send it forth saturated with prayer.

C. F. W.

Madisonville, Ky

CHAPTER 1. The Problem Of Evil

"And God saw that the wickedness of man was great in the earth, and that every imaginationofthethoughtsofhishe   artw asonlye vilcontinually ."—*Genesis vi.5.*

That we may appreciate this discussion, removed as far as possible from theological terminology and theories, and get a concrete viewpoint, the following head-lines from a single issue of a metropolitan daily will suffice: "War Clouds Hanging Low;" "Men Higher Up Involved;" "Eighty-seven Divorces On Docket;" "Blood Flows In the Streets;" "Gaunt Hunger Among Strikers;" "Arrested For Forgery;" "A White Slave Victim;" "Attempted Train Robbery;" "Kills Wife and Ends Own Life;" "Two Men Bite Dust;" "Investigate Bribery."

This fearful list may be duplicated almost every day in the year. Our land is deluged with crime, without respect to person or place; its blight touches all circles from the slum to the four hundred. Wealth and poverty, culture and ignorance, fame and obscurity, suffer alike from this Pandora Box scourge. The march of history—the pilgrimage of the race, has enjoyed but little respite from tears and blood. Those who strive to maintain a standard of purity, righteousness, and honour, are beset by strange, powerful, intangible influences, from the cradle to the grave. The child in swaddling clothes has a predisposition to willfullness, deception, and disobedience; paroxysms of passion and anger are manifested with the slightest provocation.

Notwithstanding the barriers thrown up by the home and society; the incentives and assurances for noble, industrious living, the dykes are continually giving way, so that police power and the frowning walls of penal institutions are insufficient to check the overflow. The Church of God, with its open Book, ringing out messages of life and hope at every corner; the object lessons on the "wages of sin," sweeping in full view before us, like the reel-film of a motion picture —do not seem to lessen the harvest of moral shipwreck.

According to some recent police records and statistics, only about one-half of the country's criminals are apprehended; if this is true of those who violate the law, a much smaller per cent, of those who break the perfect moral law, as related to domestic and religious life, are ever exposed. When these facts are considered, the perspective for the reign of righteousness is lurid and hopeless. The country has been amazed, recently, at the revelations of how municipal and national treasuries are being looted by extortion, extravagance, and misrule, on the part of men holding positions as a sacred trust. Civilization fosters and maintains a traffic which has not one redeeming feature; besides killing directly and indirectly more men daily than were blown up in the battle-ship *Maine.*

Let us view the problem of evil from another angle: a writer on the subject of food supplies says the earth each year furnishes an abundant quantity of fruits, meats, cereals, and vegetables to feed all her peoples; yet gaunt famine is never entirely removed. Even in America a surprising per cent, of our people are underfed and underclothed. "Fifty thousand go to bed hungry every night in New York City," declares a professor of economics. The same ratio obtains in other large cities of our land. Scenes of pinching poverty occur within a few blocks of the most wanton luxury and extravagance. One lady spends fifty thousand dollars—enough to satisfy all the hungry— on one evening's entertainment. Oranges rot on the Pacific coast by car-loads, when the children of the Ghetto scarcely taste them.

Nature fills her storehouses, and tries to scatter with a prodigal hand, but her resources are cornered and controlled by a criminal system which revolves around the "almighty dollar"—the root of all evil.

Are we to conclude that man's free agency is responsible for this moral monstrosity? Or, to be theologically particular, shall we say, free agency dominated by an innate disposition to evil: human depravity, original sin, the carnal mind? Allowing the fullest latitude to the free moral agency of the race; allowing the evil nature, like the foul soil producing a continuous crop of vile weeds, to produce an inexorable bent, or predisposition to sin, operating on man's free agency—have we a full and sufficient explanation of the presence and power of Evil?

The carnal mind is enmity with God, not subject to His laws; but the carnal mind is in competition with a *human* nature, wherein are found emotions and sentiments that are far from being all sinful: sympathy, tenderness, benevolence, paternal and filial love, sex-love, and honesty. Again, we rarely find environment as an unmixed evil. Notwithstanding these hindrances the press almost daily has details and delineations of crimes so fearful and shocking that no trace of the human appears. Frequently we hear of a man, who has committed some dreadful outrage, personified as "beast," "fiend," "inhuman," etc. A young man in his teens, wishing to marry, but being under age and without sufficient means, decided that if he could dispose of his father, mother, brother, and sister—the farm and property would all be his, then, unmolested, could consummate his matrimonial plans. Whereupon, armed with an axe, at the midnight hour, he executes his "fiendish" plot. Another man, with a young and beautiful wife, and the father of two bright children, becomes infatuated with a young woman in a distant state; he woos and wins her affections; he returns home to arrange "some business matters" on the day preceding the wedding. This business matter was to dispose of his wife and children, which he did; on the following night, led to the marriage altar an innocent, unsuspecting girl. A young minister commits double murder, and on the following day enters his pulpit and preaches from the text: "Let the words of my mouth, and the meditations of my heart, be acceptable in Thy sight, O Lord."

These cases are actual occurrences, mentioned for emphasis only, that the problem of evil may be studied from life. These examples prove conclusively that the problem goes deeper than human depravity or free agency; both are accessories—conditions, binding cords, as it were, but the jarring stroke comes from a mightier hand.

The unregenerated heart has been called a "playground," and a "coaling station " for the headmaster of all villainies. It was more than wounded pride and vanity that propagated the scheme of Haman, whereby a whole nation was to be destroyed at a single stroke.

Vengeance and hate are terrible passions, but only as they are fanned by the breath of an inhabitant of the Inferno can they go to such extremes.

It was more than a desire to crush out heresy that could instigate a "St. Bartholomew's Day," then sing the Te Deum after the bloody deed was accomplished.

We shall endeavour in the subsequent pages to throw a few rays of light, in obscure corners, on the problem of evil through its multiform phases and ramifications.

CHAPTER2.T heOriginOfE vil

"And the great dragon was cast out, that old serpent, called the Devil, and Satan, which deceiveth the whole world: he was cast out into the earth, and his angels werecastoutwithhim   ."—*Revelation xii. 9.*

It requires but a casual survey of this problem to reach a conclusion that its hideousness cannot be explained by any other hypothesis than the power of an invisible Personality. When we scrutinize the footprints of the race, it will be found that progress has been along a dark, slimy trail; the infidels and philosophers who are loud in their boastings of inherent goodness will have difficulty in reconciling this fact. All who think are confronted with an ever-recurring question— yea, exclamations: why do such things happen? What meaneth these barbarities, ravages, cruelties? Why so much domestic discord, ending in ruin—so many suicides? Why do men and women hurl themselves over the precipice of vice and deadly indulgences—when even a novice might easily see the inevitable?

For a parallel we are reminded of an incident in war: log-chains were used when the cannon-ball supply was exhausted; lanes the width of the chain length were mowed through the ranks of the opposing army. These chasms of death were closed up each time, only to be cut down again by the next discharge. The pathway of ruin is thronged—the "broad road " is easy; however, there is something stranger than this utter blindness: the victims laugh and shout on this highway, paved as it is by the macadam of crushed humanity.

Now, can there be found a rationale for this dreadful twist in human affairs—this seeming unfathomable conundrum? We cannot believe that God would create a "footstool" in which sin, suffering, and misery were to abound; no such provision could have been in the divine plan. In the Word of God alone we find the explanation of it all. The Word gives an unmistakable account of an insurrection in heaven: "Michael and his angels fought against the dragon, and the dragon fought and his angels, and prevailed not." This strange warfare was inaugurated by the great archangelic leader.

This "war in heaven" could have but one ending: the complete overthrow of the disturber and his followers. They were cast out, and are, beyond a doubt, swarming around this sin-blinded planet—invisible, yet personal and all but omnipresent. When we remember that one-third of the angelic population of heaven cast their lot with this chieftain, his strength and personality can be somewhat understood. It is written: "The tail (influence) of the dragon drew the third part of the stars (angels) of heaven, and cast them down to the earth." In their relation to heaven, the dragon and his angels met with irremediable ruin; now, defeated, humiliated, maddened, doomed, this fallen archangel and his innumerable myrmidons are filling the whole earth with every curse that can be conjured up by their superior, supernatural intelligence. There can be no room to doubt the truth of this hellish propaganda, as he is called the " god of this world."

It must be kept clearly in mind that the powers of darkness can, in no sense, mean an ethereal, impersonal spirit of evil—or perverseness of weak human nature; but rather a Being who rules and commands legions upon legions of subjects—*demons*, each of them endowed with all the powers and gifts possessed when they were ministering emissaries of God. They are now "the angels which kept not their first estate."

We have no way to estimate the size of this satanic army, marshalled for the destruction of the race and the overthrow of Christ's kingdom. However, we read in the tenth chapter of Revelation that two hundred million were turned loose in the earth at one time. Ten thousand were in the country of the Gadarenes when the Master entered there; no wonder the entire land was kept in terror, even though their incarnation seemed to have been limited to one man living in a graveyard. Seven demons were cast out of one woman.

We should keep in mind the distinction between "the devil" and demons; there is but one *Devil*, but the demons are swarming the length and breadth of the whole earth. Just as God directs His angels in ministeries of righteousness, so this god of darkness directs his angels to do his nefarious will. There are feats so daring and important that the Devil, it seems, will not trust to his underlings. He engineered in person the temptations of the Master; he entered the heart of Judas, and caused him to sell his Lord, then commit suicide.

The Bible undoubtedly teaches that Satan and his cohorts, having access to our fallen natures (which became so through his contribution of "forbidden fruit"—his great triumph in the Garden), are inciting this world to all the crimes known to our criminal dockets. Think of the train wreckers, rapists, incendiaries, white slavers, riots, strikes, grafters, gamblers, etc.; and as Paul has catalogued them: "unrighteousness, fornication, wickedness, maliciousness, envy, deceit, malignity, whisperers, backbiters, haters of God, despiteful, proud, boasters, inventors of evil things, disobedient to parents, covenant breakers, without natural affection, implacable, unmerciful."

No one can consider this long, gruesome list of iniquities without a feeling that they originated, somehow, in the realm of supernatural darkness. The worst things that can be said of fallen humanity is its availability and susceptibility to the machinations of this past master of the Pit, whose only ambition is to rob the blood of its purchase possessions by wrecking the souls for whom Christ died. Our sinful nature responds to his touch; the wonderful gamut of the soul is capable of being swept its entire length by his skill. A master player on God's greatest instrument—His masterpiece. All the fearful deeds committed seem to be acts of volition, and they are; but in the dark background lurks another superior will responsible for the initiative.

Chapter 3. Lucifer

"How art thou fallen from heaven, O Lucifer, son of the morning! How art thou cut downtothegr ound,whichdidw eakenthenations! "*—Isaiah xiv. 12.***
"And the third angel sounded, and there fell a great star from heaven, burning as it werealamp .*"—Revelation viii. 10.***
" And the fifth angel sounded, and I saw a star fall from heaven unto the earth; and tohimw asgiv enthek eyoftheb ottomlesspit .*"—Revelation ix. 1.***

It is reasonable to believe that all intelligent beings are morally free; and if free, are on probation. Intelligence, will-power, free agency, and probation are logically inseparable, regardless of place or environment. Without question, in the natural world this is true, and therefore must be true in the spiritual world. That men, angels, archangels, and redeemed spirits never attain a state of character beyond the possibility of free choice is a most fearful responsibility.

But for the imperialism of intelligent will, the *fall of angels* is unreasonable, improbable, impossible. Just how temptation can assail the inhabitants of heaven—the land, we are told, "where the wicked cease from troubling and the weary are at rest"—is beyond all human comprehension. Startling as this truth appears to be, the Bible teaches it in unmistakable language.

"Lucifer, son of the morning" an archangel, a great being, created in holiness, standing near the Throne of God. His name means "light bearer," indicative of his glorious office. We can scarcely imagine such honour, such power, such distinction. Just what the high-calling of "light bearer" was, as it was performed under the highest commission in the universe, the Book fails to tell us; but the office of Lucifer was surely the peer of Michael or Gabriel, if not above them in rank. Brilliancy and splendour radiated from his person.

May we dare, not altogether by the imagination, to venture into that remote, prehistoric time when the Second Person of the Trinity—the Anointed One—the Logos, a being of perfection, made in the image of the invisible God, became a Manifestation. That One of whom "the whole family in heaven and earth is named"; sharing the glory and honour equally with the Father, on a throne in the heaven-lies. Milton and others believe that the presence of this Manifestation aroused in Lucifer a consuming spirit of ambition and envy; he at once aspired to the place and power which God reserved for His only begotten Son.

We get still another side-light on the personality of Lucifer, when we consider his gigantic scheme. Aaron Burr planned the overthrow of his country, and dreamed of rulership; such a vision were impossible in the mind of any but a master of assemblies— an empire builder. Lucifer saw himself a ruler above that of a Creator, as "all things were made by Him." No wonder the inspired exclamation concerning him; "How art thou fallen, O Lucifer." When the climax of his overthrow came, he "fell like lightning out of heaven." The honourable cognomen is now lost forever; the glory of holiness has given place to the dishonour of despair. In the language of the poet, he "preferred to rule in hell rather than serve in heaven." This light bearer of Paradise is still a prince, but in the dark regions of endless woe; "ruler of the darkness of this world."

This archangel who felt himself capable of heavenly authority finds an easier task here below. Speaking to the Master, hear his presumption and audacity, "all these things (the kingdoms of the world, and the glory of them) will I give thee, if thou wilt fall down and worship me." What was the condition named? The restoration of what he had lost: that the Son of God pay him homage and obeisance. Baffled in this crowning stroke, he slunk away only to study the vantage more discreetly, reinforce, and reassert.

Let us keep in mind that intelligence and personality are not affected by the status of character; magnetic power and influence over others are not lost when the life is wholly given over to evil. Piety and holiness may be displaced by treachery and hate, but the force of personality remains. If any change takes place, the individual becomes more subtle and more insidious in schemes to further selfish interests. If a righteous man, endowed with unusual powers, fall into a life of sin, he carries over into his wickedness all his former gifts and faculties—nothing is lost.

This proposition enables us to further appreciate the marvellous capabilities of the fallen Lucifer. Besides the Trinity, there are none superior in the universe. God allows His enemies, both men and devils, to continue a proprietary control of their talents, whether they be one or ten. There will be no devestments until the last shifting of the scene. When we remember all the attributes, previous advantages, and present opportunities of the greatest of all apostates, the conundrum of human actions, individually and nationally, begins slowly to unravel. The fight is not alone with men in sin, but with the "prince of the powers of the air."

When Lucifer rebelled and met the just rebuke of God's wrath, all his glory, power, and brilliancy became demonized. Then, through all the millenniums there has been not one hour of relaxation; no armistice for the invisible warfare. Just as saints grow in faith, vision,and divine illumination, devils sink lower and lower; but at the same time develop in skill and efficiency by a continual application of their debased energies.

It is therefore reasonable to believe that our "common Enemy" is far more formidable than the day he was cast into the earth. Our ability to encounter him successfully becomes a more hopeless struggle with the passing days. If, in the days of Paul, it were expedient to have on the "whole armour of God" to meet him, nothing short of "all the fullness of God" is the paramount need to-day.

Chapter 4. Devil-Satan-Serpent-Dragon

"And there was war in heaven: Michael and his angels fought against the dragon; and the dragon fought and his angels, and prevailed not; neither was their place found any more in heaven. And the great dragon was cast out, that old serpent, called the Devil, and Satan, which deceiveth the whole world: he was cast out into thee arth,andhisang elsw erecastoutwithhim ."—*Revelation xii. 7-9.*

Names were significant in Bible times; they are given to-day at random, but then names were indicative of character. When character changed, the name changed: Jacob to Israel; Saul to Paul, etc. While the subject of these pages remained the holy, shining light bearer of heaven, he was Lucifer, but that name was lost to him forever. So varied were his passions, characteristics, and powers that must be known by appropriate names, and each, as given, designates some phase of his multiform personality.

Devil. Not only did Lucifer lose name and character; he exchanged a brilliant, glorious external appearance (to eyes that penetrate the invisible) for one ugly, loathsome, beastly. If language can be interpreted literally, the eye of inspiration and, revelation sees him a *Devil—sair* in the Hebrew, "hairy one," "he goat," etc. The he goat, in the Bible, stands for all that is low and base. Those who partake of the *sair* nature, in the Last Day, are called *goats*. He divided the sheep from the goats. God teaches us spiritual lessons in all nature, especially by the animal kingdom, and as the goat is a synonym for the lowest instincts of the animal; we find a being created in the highest realm of spiritual life sinking to the lowest level of brute life. If no further delineation were given—no other name than Devil— the fall was from one extreme to the other.

This cognomen carried further has a second meaning: *spoiler*, one whose touch soils and besmirches, rearranges; bright spots are smeared with black soot; flowers with sweet odour, after his blight passes over them, send out a stench; hearts of purity are defiled and debauched; faces of beauty become marred and ugly. Whenever and wherever it serves his purpose, cosmos becomes chaos. He is a spoiler.

Satan. In this familiar title we see him in the character role which dominates all his actions. As Satan he is the *hater.* Of all the evil passions of the soul, hate is the most terrible. As manifested in human relationships, the hater is a murderer. Somehow hate seems to be a resultant of wrath, malice, envy, jealousy, and revenge. Hatred in the bosom of the weak or cowardly affects only its possessor; but hatred burning in the soul of one who is strong and courageous, nothing belonging to the object of his hatred is secure: life, personal property, or reputation.

We want carefully to note the full significance of hatred; then place beside it the one who hates—yes, as no other being in all the universe can hate. He is the father of haters; the tragedies of all kinds, filling the world with terror, because of murders, bomb explosions, incendiaries, poisonings, are but the scattered rays reflected and deflected from this full orb of hate as he revolves in his sphere of darkness.

Satan hates God, hates the Holy Ghost, but the full force of his hate, of necessity, is directed towards the *Son* of God, his rival for place and power. The supreme work of the Son was the Atonement; now, the interest and anxiety of heaven has been transferred to this planet. The supreme triumph of the Second Person of the Trinity was accomplished on the Cross where He paid the price of human redemption. His energies are now directed to the breaking down of all that was accomplished on the Cross. Every movement, every motive, every virtue, coming directly or indirectly from the merits of the Atonement, become at once the object of satanic hatred. Therefore every inch of territory conquered by the gospel propaganda was and is a victory over his hateful protest.

Serpent. At the very suggestion of this title our nature recoils. The "nachash," and "zachal," mean *"fearful"—"creeper"* therefore a fearful creeper. The snake is the most repulsive and dangerous of all reptiles. There is a strange antipathy about a snake; his nature is so still, so sneaking, so oily; the appearance of one produces an involuntary shudder. Who has not felt the disgust at seeing men and women —"charmers"—take a number of the sleek, slimy monsters from a cage, and wind them around arms, neck, and body? The horror felt towards the snake is not an accident; it was in the guise of a serpent the downfall of the race was accomplished.

Men and women who are subtle, smooth, deceitful, treacherous, secretive are called "snakes in the grass." Their plans and movements are under cover; they strike or sting from an hidden covert. The serpent is synonymous with the hiss, the blazing eye, the forked tongue, the poison; once it catches the eye of a bird the poor thing may wail and flutter, but it is powerless to escape. The bird is drawn into the jaws of death by a strange magnetism.

This enemy of God and race is a serpent, slipping cautiously, noiselessly through all the dark, tangled mysteries about us. No one can fathom or interpret his cunning movements; we are stung, poisoned, charmed, fastened in the slimy coils, and yet do not know it. We have most to fear from the enemy who operates in the dark.

This fallen archangel is never so dangerous as when acting in the personification of a serpent.

Dragon. In the Hebrew it is "tannoth" *howler— jackal;* making a noise like the howling jackal in the wilderness. Again we are appalled at this title. The dragon is represented as a monstrous animal having the form of a serpent, with crested head, wings, and tremendous claws; ferocious and dangerous. The Scriptures have appropriated this fabulous monster—believed to have existed in days of mythology as the most dreaded creature on land or sea— to enforce and emphasize the danger of him who seeks our destruction. He is called the "great red dragon" —or fiery dragon, howling like a vicious jackal.

It was in this peculiar manifestation that he stood before the woman and sought to destroy the Man Child as soon as He was born; then cast a flood after her as she fled from his presence. The dragon incarnates himself, and King Herod at once seeks to destroy the infant Jesus (Matt. ii.; Rev. xii. 1-5).

Chapter 5. Diabolus-Demonia-Abaddon-Apollyon

"Then shall he say also unto them on the left hand, Depart from me, ye cursed, into everlastingfir e,pr eparedforthede vilandhisang els."—*Matthew xxv. 41.*

"And they had a king over them, which is the angel of the bottomless pit, whose name in the Hebrew tongue is Abaddon, but in the Greek tongue hath his name Apollyon."—*Revelation ix. 11.*

We now desire to analyze more minutely the Greek names Diabolus and Demonia; reference was made to this distinction in a former chapter. In the Authorized Version the two names are often translated or rather interchangeably; devil for demon, and vice versa. We read of a "legion of devils," "seven devils," "cast out devils," "possessed with devils," etc. Technically—literally translated, these statements are incorrect. Demonia should never read devil—but *demon*; diabolus always means, not a devil, but *the Devil.*

Dicibohis. This name designates him more as to his ruling and authority than to the elements of his character. We have noticed already the meaning of Devil, but from the original word we get more explicit meaning as to his rank of authority. As Lucifer we do not know his ruling rank, but in his lost estate he ranks as Commander-in-chief. Whatever we may say of him, the prefix, " arch," designating his angel rank, can be logically attached: archspoiler —archdeceiver—archaccuser—archslanderer, etc.

However, if accurately defined, diabolus means *Calumniator*—archcalumniator; a propagator of calumny. Acting in the capacity of calumniator, he seeks out and defames the innocent. He sends out a million rumours daily which would be, if tangible, cases for libel in any court.

Demonia. A demon—a fallen angel—evil spirit, an imp. Literally, a *shade*—a dark spot, moving as noiselessly and rapidly as a shadow. The many references in the New Testament to "devil," and "devils" should always be *demons;* the great multitude, so often found in one place, come from the innumerable concourse which constitute the " powers of darkness." Shadow spirits, men and women who are controlled by these dark, shadowy imps, "love darkness rather than light because their deeds are evil." The transformation, as we learned, which took place with Lucifier was just as great and radical with his angel followers; the difference was only that of degree of rank.

Abaddon-Apollyon. We have coupled the Hebrew and Greek names together, as each means exactly the same. We call the attention of the reader to the variety of names, all of which are so nearly alike, but convey a significant difference. Abaddon-Apollyon means *destroyer.* He has been discussed as a "spoiler," but one who destroys carries the work farther than the spoiler. As Abaddon or Apollyon he is the king of the abyss, or "Bottomless Pit," and when he appears it is with purpose and equipment for destruction. Just as God sent the "Destroying Angel " throughout Egypt, bringing a curse upon Pharaoh for his hardness of heart, this mighty messenger of the Abyss visits his destruction wherever and whenever he finds, not the absence of the typical blood upon the door, but when he finds it, or any evidence of allegiance to the One whose sacrificial blood he seeks to destroy.

As Abaddon-Apollyon he assumes the part of Finisher of his task; when we see him a *destroyer,* we have a full-sized photograph— leaving out not a single line of countenance, or a single character or attribute of his composite nature. He may soil, spoil, deceive, traduce, accuse, slander, wound, etc., but the ultimate aim is destruction. When sin is finished it bringeth forth death. We see how the two great Rivals stand over against each other in their respective spheres: "For this cause the Son of God was manifested, that He might destroy the works of the devil." With the same degree of purpose, the Devil seeks to destroy the work of the Son of God.

The Devil seeks to destroy truth, righteousness, virtue, religion, hope, faith, visions of God, power of the Blood, thoughts of eternity and heaven. Every beautiful, holy thing on earth he would destroy, leaving behind only black, charred cinders where once were the flowers of Eden. Just as he destroyed the earthly Paradise in the long ago, so he would blot from our hopes and aspirations the Paradise of the soul. His ambition and supreme joy would be to turn this world over to God blighted and wrecked by his finishing touches, while hell echoed with triumphant shouts—an infernal jubilee. Abaddon-Apollyon: archdestroyer.

CHAPTER 6. THE DEVIL A "BLOCKADE"

"Wherefore we would have come unto you, even I Paul, once and again; but Satan hindered us .*"—i Thessalonians ii. 18.*

"But the prince of the kingdom of Persia withstood me one and twenty days; but, lo, Michael, one of the chief princes, came to help me   .*"—Daniel x. 13.*

We find another striking interpretation couched in the title of devil. The Church in its organization is called *militant*, because it is engaged in a moral and religious warfare. The writings of Paul bristle with military terms, as two mighty armies are contending and contesting for dominion. Each army is fighting under a leader; the surging campaign has changed its base of operation—the battle-field has been transferred from heaven to this planet. The rivalry between Christ and Satan has, many times, changed *modus operandi*, but the spirit of the contest and the end—all for which they contend—change not.

The title-word of this chapter is not a Bible term; we appropriate and accommodate it because of its military meaning. Strictly in keeping with the use of terms, the "blockade" belongs to naval operations; but any movement, reconnoitre, or counter-march, which interferes, hinders, or hedges up the way of progress, is a blockade. A campaign ends in failure because of obstructions thrown up, access to base of supplies cut off, reinforcements thwarted in reaching the scene of activities, etc., convey the idea set forth in the key Scriptures used giving emphasis to the chapter heading.

The Apostle Paul had all the advantages of equipment; his intellectual attainments the very best; he was a recognized leader of men, a chosen vessel of the Lord, and full of the Holy Ghost. No man besides the Master was more able to withstand the opposition of the "prince of darkness." Yet Satan actually prevents him from going to

Thessalonica to comfort and strengthen the struggling church at that place— literally hedges up the way.

A careful examination of the tenth chapter of Daniel gives us a conversation between the prophet and a "voice,"—a "vision"—having an appearance "like the similitude of the sons of men"; evidently an angel of high rank, whose mission was to encourage Daniel, but he also acknowledges that the "prince of Persia" hindered him from coming twenty days. This mighty angel, it seems, was helpless trying to reach Daniel, until Michael came upon the scene. It was Michael who led the triumphant battle against him when he was overthrown in heaven. He alone was able to meet the "prince of Persia," the *Devil*.

We can, therefore, understand how successfully Satan can hinder— blockade the progress of righteousness wherever he chooses to concentrate his depraved energies. Volumes would be required to record the worthy enterprises in the Church of God which went down in failure, yet with no tangible explanation. Sudden reverses, turning the whole current of affairs, are daily happenings; revival efforts to reach certain communities, certain individuals, find insurmountable hindrances. It is the work of the "blockade."

Such occurrences are generally regarded as "unfortunate coincidents" rather than a resultant of some deep-laid plans— invisible and impersonal. A baby cries at a critical moment, a dog creates an uproar, the fire-bell rings, the engine becomes disabled; landslides, swollen streams, sudden illness, and many others similar, which are never credited to the proper source or cause. The Bible concedes to Satan the dignity of being the god of this- world; therefore he must of necessity control, to some extent, the physical phcnomcna, dirccting thcm to an advantage. We do not venture a dogmatic position as to what extent the hindrances in the physical world are due to his power; but the Bible most clearly teaches that he is an obstructionist.

There are hundreds of ways and places where moral and religious blockades obtain. It would seem that in the blaze of the last century of civilization war would be impossible. Why could not our Civil War have been averted? In the retrospect, we can see how easily it might have been settled without such horror and bloodshed. The Hague with its millions of endowment is grinding away on international troubles, yet arbitration fails more often than it succeeds. But war continues, and all efforts in that direction generally meet a "stone wall of opposition."

Must we conclude that all these lapses, coming in direct conflict with human weal and happiness, are just "happen-sos"? Unthinkable! "Satan hindered," declares the great apostle. "The prince of Persia withstood me twenty and one days," says the angel.

Chapter 7. The Great Magician

From the earliest records of history men have lived who seemed to possess strange, occult powers. Magicians—performing miracles, setting aside, apparently, well-known physical laws. Moses met the sorcerers and magicians of Egypt in close competition. There are men to-day, on lecture platforms, performing feats which are miracles; there seems to be no visible explanation.

"The hand is quicker than the eye," it is said; watches are pounded to pieces before your eyes, the fragments crammed into a gun; the gun is discharged, and the watch will be hanging on a hook, running as if nothing had happened. We once saw a man sewed up in a tarpaulin, placed in a huge trunk, and the trunk strapped securely. In less than five minutes the man came out from an enclosure where the trunk was placed; not one buckle loosened, and not one stitch in the tarpaulin broken. Cannonballs are taken from hats; live ducks, rabbits, and a dozen tin vessels are drawn from one hat in rapid succession. Cards are made to jump out of the deck when called by name. One magician laid his assistant on a table, cut off his head with a large knife, lifted the gory head by the hair and placed it on another table; then carried on a conversation with the severed head in the presence of the astonished audience.

Every one knows these wonderful feats are done by some kind of magic, but for all we can see they are done; the most astute observer cannot detect the secret. The Apostle exhorts the believers to put on the whole armour of God, to be able to stand (not to be swept away or captured) against the wiles of the Devil. Then the Devil is a trickster—a sleight-of-hand performer—a magician. One of his many methods to accomplish his purpose, we find, is delusion: practicing sleights, tricks, and works of magic on the gullibility of his victims.

How many unsophisticated men and boys have been robbed in daylight on a street corner by some little "game," or trick, by a sharper. Farms have been deeded away for nothing in return. Now, if we were to catalogue all the tricks of all the conjurers of all ages, we have in this evil chieftain a consummation, an embodiment of them all; he is not only a magician, but the chief of them. He incessantly seeks victims more astutely than the crook seeks the ignorant with a purpose of robbery. Observe the text says, "wiles of the devil"; not one, but many; while we are penetrating and avoiding one of his "wiles," behold, we are in the meshes of another. Human intellect cannot fathom the feats of magic performed in friendly entertainment, where every opportunity is given to examine—then how much more are we at the mercy of seances concocted, not to entertain, but to delude and capture.

The astrologers, soothsayers, and magicians; the clairvoyants, ancient and modern, are insignificant compared with this great magician. Is he not superior and supernatural, possessed with unearthly powers? Are there any combinations and hidden laws of which he is unacquainted? Besides, no one is more familiar with the weaknesses and susceptibility of human nature than he. So astute and cunning are his "wiles tricks of magic—Paul seems to feel that only the girdings and enduements of God, giving spiritual illumination to the things invisible, can withstand them. The antithesis of the Apostle's exhortation leaves no doubt in our mind as to his meaning: if we strive and contend in our own wisdom, deception and defeat are inevitable.

To be explicit, does it not look as if multitudes are under a delusion—seeing things through distorted and false lenses—when words and actions, by the best and truest people on earth, are seen as blatant hypocrisy?

Does it not look as if a sleight-of-hand expert were manipulating the ideals of this pleasure-mad generation; hiding the true character and dangers which lurk in every indulgence and excess? "Presto, veto—change;" there you are, safe, satisfied, happy. "Spirits of devils," declares the seer of Patmos, "working miracles, going to the kings, and to the whole world." The arena wherein he practices his deadly delusions is the whole world.

No places exempt; no peoples immune. The whole armour of God is the only sure protection.

CHAPTER 8. THE ROARING LION

Thus far we have studied Diabolus under various titles and cognomens which deal almost exclusively with the secret side of his nature: the propaganda of hidden arts. The caption of this chapter will indicate quite a different proposition. This title swings him into full view, stripped of all deception and legerdemain. The lion walks up and down the earth, showing no quarters, making no apologies for his presence. When he roams in the forests, he is king; he allows no beast to interfere or question his rights, and none dare to do it. He kills, tears to pieces, and devours whatever he can catch; his roar strikes terror to all the forest dwellers.

The lion, therefore, is noisy; his approach is with loud demonstration. There is something in noise that weakens and frightens; the keen clap of thunder, the shout of an approaching army, the blast of ram's horns, the loud proclaiming of the sword of the Lord and Gideon are historical examples of victories by noise. The lion is also powerful; no other beast has a chance in a match with him. One stroke with his mighty paw is death. He walks about conscious of his strength; an ox or a buffalo are no more his equal than a mouse contending with a cat. The lion is vicious; his going forth has one definite object— "seeking to devour."

The lion presupposes that all the earth belongs to him; deer, antelopes, panthers, buffaloes, horses, cattle, etc., have no rights or possessions of which he feels under the slightest obligation to respect. The Devil does not come out *in person:* hoofs, horns, claws, bushy mane—the make-up of a lion, building up his kingdom by tearing down and destroying men and institutions opposed to him. He does these things, as a lion, by incarnating himself in men, evil combines, corrupt politics, vicious society, the liquor traffic, the White Slave system, etc. As he appropriates and embodies these institutions by entering in and possessing the men who are leaders, he no longer acts as a conjurer or snake, but a *Lion*. The fullness of the earth, and they that dwell therein, belong to him, to use, desecrate, prostitute, kill, devour, or destroy, just so he may best serve and satisfy his insatiable appetite. Cities are to be officered and governed, not for the peaceful protection of their citizens, but for plunder, boodle, and graft. Men who desire to be public servants in deed and in truth must fight "a roaring lion." The man who steps to the front with a desire to question and curtail the exploitations of the "officials," the "traffic," the "gang", places his life at once in imminent peril. Threats, black hand letters, pistols, poison, bombs, and torches are the instruments boldly used to destroy the man or men who do not believe that these human lions should be allowed to filch and devour the privileges and possessions of others.

We find our "adversary, the devil, as a roaring lion, walking about, seeking whom he may devour," has three methods which he uses according to the exigencies of the case. It is first a "roar," a bluff, or bulldoze: the threat of the "boss," whether he be a political boss, an ecclesiastical boss, or a liquor boss, accomplishes wonders in coercion; it frightens and cowers the weak-kneed and backboneless. The crack of the slave-driver's whip brought the obstreperous negro into humble submission. Men in office, in pulpits, in editorial rooms, have been awed into silence by the roar of men "higher up." Then truth, righteousness, justice, and conscience are crucified; and behind the scene leering devils hold a jubilee of triumph.

However, the bluff and bulldoze will not always succeed; and when these loud, but mild methods fail, the boycott is ordered. Those who can stand undaunted in the presence of roaring threats will quail before the prospects of financial ruin. Employees are discharged, patronage cut off, positions given to others, preachers asked to resign. Somehow evil is so compactly organized, wires of connection are so completely in touch with every nook and corner, that the "boss" sits quietly at the switchboard and issues orders. The "big stick" and boycott have carried many elections; municipal, state, and national; they have made merchandise of sovereignty, and bargain counters of conscience. "Your clerk must take his name off that petition, or we will withdraw our patronage;" "His wife is an active worker in the W. C. T. U.—you must discharge him," were the identical words overheard in a private office. Business and public men dread the boycott. Behind the boycott is our "adversary, the Devil."

But the bluff and boycott by no means mark the limit when the self-assumed rights and privileges of the lion are questioned. Few can rise above the threat and intimidation; but the roaring activities of the boss will not always suffice. The lion in corrupt politics, in evil traffics, in priestly bigotry and intolerance, will not hesitate to stab, shoot, or burn to get rid of an offensive opposer. It is not necessary to discuss facts so well known as these; but we are investigating the sources; we want to locate the bacilli rather than examine the pustule.

We wish to reiterate a previous statement; the "roaring lion" is never heard if the still fight, the oily snake methods serve to a better advantage. The Apostle's exhortation is timely: "Be vigilant, be sober"—be on the alert constantly, and be at your best, as

an "adversary" who knows no boundary lines in his work of
subjugation and destruction has declared war to the end.

CHAPTER 9. AN ANGEL OF LIGHT

"For such are false apostles, deceitful workers, transforming themselves into the apostles of Christ. And no marvel; for Satan himself is transformed into an angel oflight ."—*2 Corinthians xi. 13-14.*

The Devil is a person, with a great personality; but like human beings, he is not equally endowed in all the attributes of his nature. However, the Book gives us no information as to his weaknesses. He is all superlative strength; but if at any point there is a special endowed faculty that would seem to overshadow the others, it is surely manifested when Satan is transformed into an *angel of light.* The reason for this is obvious; it is a return to his old office of " light bearer." When he can effectively serve his purpose by this startling transformation—darkness to light—he is at once in a realm where he is familiar with every inch of the territory.

A close observation of the signs of the times—the happenings in social and religious circles—will reveal the fact that *light* is not only his most familiar role, but his favourite role. The world is attracted by things that are bright, beautiful, cheerful; anything that hides the sombre side of life, throws a mystic veil over its realities, and helps us to forget—whether it be books, music, lectures, or the nonentities of society—outweigh all else in the casting of accounts and in forming comparative estimates.

If Satan were allowed to pose for a full sized picture of himself, just as he wishes to be seen by the children of this generation, no portrait painter could produce a specimen of rarer beauty; it would grace the walls of the most exclusive parlour, and attract special attention in any great art gallery of the world. There would be no sharp angles, no coarse, sensuous lines, no out-of-date adornment— the traditional fiery-red would not appear, but rather the most delicate tints and shades of colour. The features would be the most graceful and artistic combination of curves and circles. The " hairy one," the jackal, the snake, the lion, the shadow, the spoiler at once become as " beautiful as a dream." Amazing transformation!

" The devil of to-day " is not only an apostle of sunshine, but of beauty. This world is full of beauty; and why should we not forever keep the ugly and distorted in the background? The development of the *beautiful* should be one of the fine arts. Think only of beauty; speak only of beauty; see only the beautiful; then the sinful and unlovely will disappear. An angel of light—how suggestive!

As an apostle of sunshine his mission is to flood the world with light, and he does it; but observe—it is *his* light; it neither warms nor illuminates, but for spectacular purposes it answers every demand. It reveals new standards of duty; proves the wrathful things in the Word of God to be spurious, and the old plan of salvation obsolete and unsuited to the present day needs. Such words as self-denial, crucifixion, dead to sin, judgment day, cross bearing, etc., so prominent in the New Testament, must not be given a literal interpretation. Such truths cast an unnecessary gloom over the souls of otherwise happy people.

" The devil of to-day " believes that ethical culture should be the slogan, the watchword, the shibboleth of every pulpit and rostrum. Religion without refinement is absurd; the esthetic taste should be looked after more than belief in some abstract Bible doctrine; then the race would be free from the bondage of creed and fear. True religion is nothing more than a just appreciation of art, literature, science, philosophy, and nature. God is in all these things rather than some musty, stereotyped statement of faith.

He further believes it is a waste of energy for women to be organizing into societies to study and help conditions among the slums or heathen lands, and urging upon the hard worked people to pay a tenth of their income to support missionaries who are better fed and housed than themselves. Far better devote the time to social clubs, book circles, euchre and bridge parties, and dressing properly.

We want to call attention again to a truth often overlooked: the Devil and demons are never satisfied in a disembodied state; when they cannot enter the souls of men, they seek something else. They will enter a swine when there is nothing better available. We believe " the prince of the air " can wield a powerful influence, unincarnated, *in the air*, but he schemes and works best when he can possess and direct intelligent flesh and blood.

Just now the machinery of the Church and all the auxiliaries are devoting their energies to various branches of social service; this is good, Christlike, and necessary; the point we raise, germane to this subject, is not the work, but the abuse of the idea: social service and humanitarianism are not religion. They are the fruits of the Good Samaritan spirit in the world, but they cannot take the place of personal relationship to God. " Though I give my body to be burned, and all my goods to feed the poor," says Paul, " it profiteth me nothing " without love—divine love. The angel-of-light gospel places the emphasis on works without faith. Love the world, enjoy its lusts and allurements, disregard all Puritanic ideals of life, be a part of all worldliness— but be kind, cheerful, optimistic, generous, benevolent: help humanity. " Pay the fiddler," then dance as you please. Do penance when your conscience lashes you; but buy indulgences by works of supererogation. " On with the dance, let joy be unconfined."

A concrete example will illustrate the proposition before us, and also reveal the power of polished, cultured emissary of " sunshine and smiles." The little city had a population of about fifteen hundred people; there were four churches of nearly equal strength. Each congregation had a large flourishing organization of young people. Scarcely any worldliness obtained—dancing and card playing rarely ever. The pious, consecrated young people attracted no little attention. Finally there came to the place a young woman fresh from college and conservatory as teacher of music and delsarte. She was an adept at all the niceties of modern society; things took on new colour at once. The work began with a literary club, then cards, then the dance. She was beautiful and magnetic; in six months the " stupid meetin's " of the League and Christian Endeavour were abandoned for things more exhilarating. The religious foundation which had been crystallizing for years among the simple hearted boys and girls gave place to the gayeties imported from the classic circles of city and college life. She moved among them " an angel of light."

CHAPTER10.T heSo werOfT ares

" The kingdom of heaven is like a man that sowed good seed in his field: but while men slept, his enemy came and sowed tares among the wheat and went away."—*Matthew xiii. 24-25.*

" The field is the world; the good seed are the children of the kingdom; but the tares are the children of the wicked one; the enemy that sowed them is the devil."—*Matthew xiii. 38-39.*

The parable of the Sower is one of common-sense appeal; the sensible farmer sows only good seed. The growing of tares among the wheat is not in the original plan. Good seed were sown, but behold the tares! Whence came they? While the servants slept an Enemy came and sowed them. The Master gives us His own interpretation: He is the sower—the good seed are the children of the kingdom, men and women into whose hearts the Truth has entered—the converted part of the Church. The sleeping of the servants is the unwatchfulness of the Church: coldness, indifference, backslidden. The Enemy seizes the opportunity—the carelessness of Christ's servants—and sows *bad seed.* The enemy is the Devil—the Wicked One; the bad seed are the children of the Devil. Growing side by side in this world-field are the children of God and the children of the Devil.

The tare, or cheat, in appearance resembles the wheat; it grows exactly the same height, and viewed casually, or at a distance, cannot be detected from the genuine. Only the threshing and sifting bring out the difference. These tares are the propaganda of the Devil, but a perfect imitation of the children of the kingdom. They make a profession, adhere to the same rules and regulations, profess and maintain, outwardly, a standard of morality, wear all the regalia—even particular about details. We observe another striking resemblance: strange as it may seem, these tares—children of the Devil—seek as their guide no books of heathen philosophy, or twentieth century atheism; they make great capital of the Bible; the ceremonies and ordinances are carried out to the letter. On a day of dress parade and review they meekly grade A 1.

Such an inconsistency is so glaring as to be almost unthinkable; but the parable teaches it beyond a doubt. The Devil sows into the Church his children: *a corrupt profession of Jesus Christ.* In a former chapter we studied the Devil as a *destroyer;* and it will be remembered that in a preceding parable he came as a vulture devouring the seed; now he seeks to further weaken and hinder by adulteration. While continuing the battering-ram process from without, a reversed method is used; he scales the ramparts and places his cohorts on the inside, and, wherever possible, assumes leadership in a campaign of self-destruction. We are amazed at such audacity, but the Master, who is a rival in the field, has illuminated the parable for us.

There is a note of optimism ringing out in the land to the effect that the day of triumph is at hand; doors are opening, walls are crumbling, conservative nations are studying our religion, municipalities are being renovated, higher standards in public life are demanded, the Church is lifting the race out of superstition and prejudice—we are about to see a " nation born in a day." What does it mean? It means that Satan is being chained—defeated, etc. This sounds good and plausible; but a closer inspection will reveal, not a retreat, not an armistice, not a victory, but a *change of base.*

Twenty years ago a leading teacher said: " Unless the signs of the times fail, the true Church of Christ is about to enter upon the most serious struggle of her history. She is no longer called merely to fight an open foe without, but as Dr. Green, of Princeton, says, ' the battle rages around the citadel/ and she is forced to fight the traitors within. The real enemy is to be found on the inside." If such a condition were true then, what is it to-day, since the last two decades have been the most revolutionary in the history of the Church on the line of skepticism and advanced thought?

The *Free Thinkers' Magazine* recently had this to say: " Tom Paine's work is now carried on by the descendants of his persecutors; all he said about the Bible is being said in substance by orthodox divines, and from chairs of theology." Another writer observes: " No need of Bridlaughs and Ingersols wasting time preaching against the early chapters of Genesis, sneering at the story of temptation, cavilling at the record of long lives, denying the confusion of tongues, doubting if not denying the deluge, when Christian ministers, on account of their official position, are doing the same work more effectually."

" Freedom of thought in religion," said an orthodox preacher at Tom Paine's one hundredth anniversary, " just what he stood for, is what most of us have come to. In his own day vilified as an atheist—to-day he is looked upon as a defender of just principles of faith." There is a wide range of opinions found in the growing crop of tares: some are literalists, touching Biblical interpretation, getting the minutia of husks, but rejecting the kernel—the envelope, but missing the message; others remain in the Church, preach a gospel shelter under her roof—eat her bread, but deny the supernatural *in toto.* Few, if any, are honest enough to step out.

The Devil prefers his *cheat* to grow in the same soil prepared for the wheat. No place is so wholesome and convenient for the children of the Devil as inside the Church of God. Why is not the wrath of God poured out on the children of the Devil who have assumed place and power in His Church? The same processes used for the removal of the tares would injure and uproot some of the wheat. There is now no remedy; at an unguarded moment the harm was done. The Enemy continues to enter every available door, sowing, sowing, sowing— beside all waters. Not until the angelic reapers thrust in their sickles for the harvest will the children of the Devil cease to occupy, influence, and control.

CHAPTER 11. T hEAr chSlanderer

" For God doth know that in the day ye eat thereof, then your eyes shall be opened, andy eshallb easg ods,kno wingg oodande vil.*"—Genesis iii.5.*

" But put forth thine hand now and touch all that he hath, and he will curse thee to thyface .''—*Job i. 11.*

It is the first scene of the human drama; the staging is in an earthly Paradise; perfection is written on everything animate and inanimate. With but one restriction man roams through Edenic beauties, a being " good and very good," happy and holy. His communion with God is unbroken; fountains of love are opened in his heart as he beholds the beautiful mate at his side. Our wildest imaginations cannot estimate the glories of that life-morning; but behold the Serpent. He utters his first words in the scheme of ruin, and it is a slander against God. " Aha, He knows if you eat you will be like He is—knowing all things, be as gods; He is not treating you fairly; the case is misrepresented. You will not die, but you will be wise. Why does He keep back such privileges from you? " As a result of this slander, the Paradise is lost. Flowers, fruits, peace and plenty are exchanged for weeds, briers, toil, sweat, suffering, death.

Again we find his impudent presence on the day Job is offering sacrifices. Reading between the lines, we can imagine a conversation like this: " You here? You are looking for some pretense to discount My people; you say none are good—all hypocrites. What do you think of My servant Job? What have you to say about him? "

" Oh, of course," says the slanderer, " you have him hedged around—blessing him continually. It pays Job to be good; just take away your special care of his material welfare and see—he will curse Thee to Thy face"

An artist once painted a picture of the human tongue in a way to represent his conception of how the " tongue of slander " should appear. It was long, coiled like a serpent, tapering at the end into a barbed spear point; from each of the papilla, scarcely visible, was a needle point, from which oozed a green, slimy poison. The slandering tongue is " a fire, a world of iniquity—it defileth the whole body—it is set on fire of hell."

The slanderer is no respecter of persons; he rakes and scrapes the uttermost parts of the earth for victims: king and peasant, rich and poor, priest and prophet; living or dead suffer alike when once this vile, inhuman spirit touches them. Bacon said: " Calumny crosses oceans, scales mountains, and traverses deserts with greater ease than the Scythian Abaris, and, like him, rides on a poisoned arrow." The winds of the Arabian desert not only produce death, but rapid decomposition of the body; so doth slander destroy every virtue of human character. The cloven-hoof slanderer, like the filthy worm, leaves behind a trail of offal and stench though his pathway wind through a bower of earth's sweetest flowers. A writer has said: " So deep does the slanderer sink in the murky waters of degradation and infamy that, could an angel apply an Archimedian moral lever to him, with heaven as a fulcrum, he could not in a thousand years raise him to the grade of a convict felon."

" Whose edge is sharper than a sword; whose tongue

Out-venoms all the worms of Nile; whose breath

Rides on the posting winds, and doth belie

All corners of the world; kings, queens, and states,

Maids, matrons, nay, the secrets of the grave

This viperous slander enter."

Iago is said to be the greatest villain in fiction or history; the revolting crimes of Herod—slaughtering the innocent—does not compare with Iago. Herod saw in the Man Child a possible rival, and blinded by jealousy and ambition, he becomes the most heartless murderer—of all times. But what was the crime of Iago? Slander! With no object in view, no advantage to gain, and too much of a coward to make an open charge, he slanders by insinuation the beautiful Desdemona until the enraged Othello strangles her to death.

How can we reconcile this base passion in human character, as slander has no other avenue of expression? It is unnatural, inhuman, and hellish. The wolf and tiger devour to satisfy hunger; the vulture eats and fattens on rotting carcases, but the slanderer does neither. With the blood cruelty of a savage beast, the degraded appetite of the scavenger, the destroyed victims of fiendish passion only intensify and burn, but never satisfy the slanderer. This spirit was never born among men; its origin is the region of the damned, where hunger gnaws, thirst fires, lust arouses, revenge consumes—but satisfaction is unknown. The hot breath of slander comes from a bourne where dead hopes spring up eternal.

The caption of the chapter denominates the Devil as the arch slanderer; we use it because there is no word of sufficient strength to convey the idea; " arch " fails to convey the whole truth in this case. Archangel is an intelligible term, as there are many of high order; there is, however, but One slanderer. Just as he is the " father of liars "—propagating all lies—his relation to liars does not admit of comparison. He slandered from the day of his fall; he is the father of slanderers. Whether it be circulated in the " submerged world' the quiet circles of church life, or among the " Four Hundred " of fashion —it is a deflected arrow from the one great quiver.

No being—holy men, angels, or the Son of God— can escape the tongues dripping the venom of slander through the subtle incarnation of that fountainhead of every evil suggestion or insinuation. Whatever destroys happiness, creates doubt and suspicion among the people, ending in litigation, divorces, and murders, fulfills the mission of slander. The caldron from which exudes this vile stench—filling all the earth—is seething and boiling in the Bottomless Pit, or wherever the throne of his majesty—the Devil— is located. The society of earth will never be free from the poison of evil-speaking until the Archslanderer is arrested, chained, and located in the penitentiary prepared for him from the foundation of the world.

CHAPTER 12. THE DOUBLE ACCUSER

" Hast not thou made an hedge about him, and about his house, and about all that hehathone veryside?thouhastblesse dthew orkofhishands,andhissubstanceis increasedintheland ."—*Job i. 10.*

"Now is come salvation, and strength, and the kingdom of our God, and the power of his Christ: for the accuser of our brethren is castdown, which accused them beforeourGo ddayandnight."— *Revelation xii.10.*

When we consider the Diabolus character—his strength and opportunity, whereby he visits his vengeance upon a weak, susceptible race, we can readily understand that his make-up would be far from complete without a continuous outflow of slander. But his courage and audacity stand out in glaring relief when we find him an Accuser. It does not require large intelligence or bravery to be a slanderer—only baseness of character—but to be an accuser, face to face with false charges, especially in the presence of One who has power over all things, reveals an impudent bravery that dazes the judgment.

When questioned of God about his presence among devout spirits—as they were assembled for worship—he answered in the manner of a guilty boy: "Just going to and fro in the earth." Peter tells us that his mission of going to and fro is of seeking and devouring. He is then reminded of Job's character-how that this saint is perfect and just; Satan's blighting influence has not been able to touch and overthrow the aged Job. In his shrewd rejoinder Satan accuses God of two sins: *partiality and falsehood.*

Translated into its literal meaning, the language would be about as follows: " I deny that Job is perfect; but for the protection you have thrown around him he would be as other men. His pretended piety is hypocrisy; he serves you because you have blest him with abundance; he has not fallen into sin because you have hedged him about. If you treated Job as you treat others, his holiness would soon be about as genuine as mine."

Satan accuses God of protecting His servant and blessing him in material things in a special and partial manner, viz: " a respecter of persons." But the fiercest accusation is hidden in his reply to God's question, also put in the form of a question, and finished by an emphatic declaration: Job is not the man God said he was; " but put forth Thine hand and touch all that he hath, and he will curse Thee to Thy face." A being who can stand before the Lord God, of whom the hosts of heaven sing and shout— he, himself, once among the number—saying: " Holy, Holy, Holy," and accuse Him of being guilty of partiality and falsehood—what may *we* expect from him? The Word says he accuses the saints day and night.

Observe that he accuses the *saints*, those who are striving in righteousness. The man who lies, cheats in business, accumulates a fortune, and lives all the vices without apology is not an object of malicious accusation. The scandals in select circles cause only a ripple, even though the offenses occupy much space of the associated press. The principles of such affairs are often staged as heroes and heroines for the entertainment of a morbid public taste. Satan accuses the saints; the presumption is shouted from the housetops: " There is none that doeth good, no not one."

The saints—every good man and woman—must at some time face charges against their moral or religious character. This hellish machination goes on day and night. It is reasonable to conclude that much of the unrest, depression, and backslidings among the people of God may be traced to this cause; innocent men and women have not only cast away their hope through rumoured accusations, but have been driven to desperation and suicide.

The reader must keep in mind the suggestion made in a former chapter: that while Satan has the power by his presence of himself, or his minions, to create an atmosphere, unfathomable, impenetrable, yet surcharged with horror and dread; but his activities are seldom apart from human instrumentalities. Just as he is the arch slanderer, through the word of mouth, so is he the accuser, both of God and saints, through human personalities under his control.

A flood sweeps away, or lightning destroys a man's possessions; he looks up, curses and accuses God of cruelty and injustice. Death enters the home; the mourners charge God falsely. His accusations are confined to no particular method; the one most suited to the case is used, whether self-condemnation or from another. Self-reproach, through memory and meditation, is a most powerful agency in carrying on this work. Once we begin to think on our ways—seeking to turn our steps unto the testimony of God —we face a life of sins and blunders mountain high and unsurmountable. But when faith takes wings and lifts the agonizing soul " out of the mire and clay," an everlasting reminder of the *past* clings to us, often robbing us of peace and joy. How many Christians have grown weary and given up because of memories blackened by consequences of past sins —sins which God said, if we confess and forsake, He would " remember them against us no more forever."

If the truth, which can never be revealed until the Judgment Day, could be known! Our asylums are swarming with unfortunates who have lost mental balance because of remorse and condemnation, resulting from an accusing memory. Wherever Satan is unable to lure the saints into actual transgression their life and usefulness are often destroyed by tormenting spirits accusing them day and night. The Book holds out no deliverance from this scourge until the Accuser is forever cast down by the wrath of God at the final shifting of the scene.

CHAPTER 13. SATAN A SPY

And the Lord said unto Satan, Whence comest thou? Then Satan answered the Lord, and said, From going to and fro in the earth, and from walking up and down in it."—*Job i. 7.*

The spy is the most dangerous man in the army; more is he to be feared than the genius of a Napoleon or a Lee. The sphere in which he operates has no duplicate in military activities; his bravery, boldness, and daring are unexcelled. Whether he be called from the ranks, or from among the commissioned officers, his counsel and suggestions get a hearing in the highest commandery of the army.

The movements of a spy are unknown even to his own corps, much less to the enemy. After receiving authority for such a perilous undertaking he is a free lance, going and coming at will. Not only does he go beyond the enemy's line, but mingles freely with them in the camp. There is nothing in his appearance to indicate who or what he is. To-day he is a civilian peddling fruits among the soldiers, or innocently driving a yoke of steers along the street or country road; to-morrow he is within the camp, dressed in their gay uniform, familiar with passwords and countersigns. Then he appears as a decrepit old woman, seeking a son who " run away to jine the solgers." In a few hours he is quietly resting or joking with the boys of his own regiment.

When a spy is captured all military courtesies are set aside; he is not even allowed the honour of a court-martial; but without trial he is executed at once.

It is of special interest, in view of the application to our subject, to notice the particular business of a spy. Just as his movements are unknown, so is his mission unknown. He hurries to and fro, gathering up such bits of information here and there as he deems important for the cause he represents. If he belongs to the Federal forces he appears clothed in the " butternut gray "; then by tactics of bravery and nerve he enters the Confederate gray lines. The slightest blunder is certain death. He takes a mental inventory of the whole situation, but in such a way as to attract the attention of no one. The strength of the fortifications, the size and number of the batteries, the commissary department, and the chances and probabilities of reinforcements. In a moment, under the cover of night, he fades out into the darkness and is gone. The budget of information is placed at the earliest possible moment into the war councils of his own army.

Satan plays the role of a crafty spy; he has access, by some mysterious power, to the heart life of men. At no point of the game for immortal trophies is he so dangerous as when he can take advantage because of his secret knowledge of men's weaknesses and sins. Only a vicious degenerate can be tempted into all the crimes known to the docket of the Bible; few beings on this planet but are fortified at some point of character. They may be weak in many ways —but early training or environment have helped them to become strong in some particulars.

The spy seeks to know when and where a blow may be struck in the enemy's lines, at a place of least resistance. The soul battles are exactly the same; we have no special battles where we are strong; things that might overcome another will mean nothing to us. Our battles are ever fought around the points of weak fortification; the enemy rarely, if ever, has the pleasure of shouting over our downfall from the best that is in us.

The victories of athletic games—the pugilistic bouts in the sporting arena, the mortal duel with rapiers, the battle-fields where thousands fell—have been lost and won by the application of this principle. The general with his field-glass sees a weakening in the enemy's line and orders a charge; the duelist observes a shortening of breath or an awkward movement and seizes the opportunity. It is the weak link in the chain of life that breaks; sins of the lower nature —sensuality— might not appeal to some who fall an easy victim to pride, ambition, or covetousness; others who are liberal, honest to the cent, unassuming, are helpless when tempted in the realm of lower passions. We are at an incalculable disadvantage when our enemy is familiar with our vulnerable points.

So long as the heart is unregenerated and unpurified by the cleansing power of the Holy Ghost, Satan has access to every nook and corner of our heart life. He enters and discovers every vulnerable and invulnerable section of the souls fortification. The tempted and fallen are often unable to tell how it was done. "Why did you go there?" or, "Why did you do it? " Oh, so many, many times do we hear the answer: " I do not know." A friend once showed me a little iron safe in which he kept his valuable papers. This safe had a very ingenious lock; the combinations were such, and the mechanism so wonderful, that it was capable of *three hundred thousand combinations.*

Why and how are sane men and women overcome? They were met at a certain place, under peculiar circumstances; met by several—a word, a smile, an argument, a pressure of the hand. How was it done? They do not know. Somehow the attack came in a way which rendered them helpless to resist. One effort failed—a dozen failed; but as often as it failed the Expert changed the *combination*, until the door yielded, and an entrance into the citadel of Mansoul was effected. *Three hundred thousand combinations.*

The spy has information from within; and, therefore, the most dangerous man in the army. Satan, by his supernatural powers directing his practice and experience for several millenniums, is a crafty, sagacious spy, acquainted with all the weaknesses and emotions of the human heart. Who is equal to such an enemy? Contending alone, *no one* on this sin-burdene d footstool.

CHAPTER14.AQU ACKDOCT OR

" Having the form of godliness, but denying the power thereof; from such turn away."—*2 Timothy iii.5.*

We do not agree with some late views of the nature of sin—that it is a physical and mental disorder: the resultant of heredity, food, soil, climate and social environment. If the root of the difficulty springs from these primary causes, the whole problem of evil could be wiped out in one generation by the application of sanitary laws and social betterment. In the Bible sin is known by several disease terms, but always such diseases as were incurable by any treatment known in those days: leprosy, born blind, deadly poison, paralytic, etc. Sin is a disease, and the whole man, body, mind, and spirit, is more or less affected therefrom; but it is, in particular, a soul malady, going deeper than human remedies can reach, whether social or medicinal.

To cure this soul disease the race has sought eagerly from the day Cain and Abel built their altars. All the ramifications of civilization have had one all-absorbing desire: a readjustment of something fundamentally wrong within. This fight for an atonement with the Creator has been a long, heart-sore pilgrimage; it has painted the blackest pages of history and committed the bloodiest crimes.

This human drama has been enacted in tragedy and tears. Why is it so? Because deeper than any other heart-throb is the consciousness of personal uncleanness, and the bitter anguish it has caused.

The dead civilizations, on their monuments and mausoleums, have left behind, carved indelibly, one story—whether on the banks of the Nile, the Areopagus of Greece, or the land of the Montezumas—it is the story of feeling in the dark after God. They had the disease and sought for a remedy. From the days of the astrologers and soothsayers, anxious souls have been victimized by every fad, fake and fanaticism in their search for relief. The venders of pulverized snake skins and lizard tongues, in their day, found as willing a patronage as the cultured proprietors of sanitariums to-day. The long-haired man on a goods box can do a flourishing business, if he has the gift of gab to convince the crowd his stuff will *cure*.

The quack doctor does not handle a variety of medicine; he knows just enough of anatomy and materia medica to make his speech sound scholarly— but his remedy, costing less than the price of one visit from a physician, will cure all the ills of the human body. Like De Soto, we are seeking the fountain of perennial youth—the elixir of life.

Just as the disease of the body and a passion to live open wide the door to charlatans, fakirs, and " healers " claiming powers direct from Gabriel to Beelzebub, so the disease of the soul, and a hunger for eternal life—" deep calling unto deep "—has opened the door of the heart to the religious doctor with his cure-all prescriptions. Out from unknown depths comes the yearning for readjustment and reconciliation with God.

No being, beside the Godhead, is more familiar with the secret hopes and impulses of the soul—than Satan. The long-haired quack on the street, bawling his "junk," is not half so anxious to defraud the crowd as Satan is to prescribe remedies that will not cure. His chief aspiration is to flood the land with bogus treatments which not only fail to cure, but they preempt the disease-infected spots so as to prevent the introduction of the genuine remedy.

The quack doctor is, no doubt, pleased when an imaginary cure has been wrought by his wares; but Satan is filled with wrath if some of his formulas strike deeper than he anticipated, and a soul emerges from darkness unto light. This, however, does not often occur; he is too cunning to advertise to a hungry, sin-sick world that which will bring permanent relief.

The beating of tom-toms by an upper Congo medicine man to drive away evil spirits has about the same efficacy as much that may be found in the esthetic circles of the world's religiosity. "A form of godliness" be it ever so beautiful and orderly, which does not seek and obtain the inner power is just another way of beating tom-toms.

We look with compassion upon the poor benighted heathen woman who trots around the temple of her god one hundred times on a moonlight night; but how much improvement over her plan of salvation do we find in the blaze of twentieth century Christian enlightenment, if our religion consists of just " doing something," rather than having *faith* in a power that saves through the impartation of the Holy Ghost? At no time in the history of the Church have we done so many things as we are doing now—all good; but observe: the Church and the world go hand in hand. It is a rare exception when an essential difference can be seen in the life and business methods of the professor and nonprofessor. " They will have a form of godliness," says Paul, " but deny the power."

It was not a dream or hallucination which took the rich and poor, in the long ago, out from the world and caused them to give up even their lives cheerfully; it was an application of the power. They had tested the " fountain opened in the house of David for sin and uncleanness."

' 'Oh, that fountain de ep and wide,

Flowing from the wounded side,

That was pierced for our redemption, long ago;

In thy ever cleansing wave, there is found all power to save;

It's the power that healed the nations long ago."

In the multitude of pretenses, makeshifts: forms, ceremonies, chantings, genuflections, ordinances, will worship, self-righteousness, " wondrous works,"— " form of godliness "—who is responsible? It is the great Quack Doctor that is deceiving the world; those who will not be dragged into sin and ruin he surfeits their lives with a "for m of godliness, but deny the power " plan of salvation.

Chapter 15. The Devil a Theologian

"Now the Spirit speaketh expressly, that in the latter times some shall depart from thefaith,givinghe edtose ducingspirits,anddo ctrinesofde vils."—*i Timothy iv. i.*

Theology is defined as " the science which treats of God, His existence, character, government, and doctrines," or the science of religion—a system of truth derived from the Scriptures. The caption of this article—The Devil a Theologian—-jars our spiritual nerve centres. There are three things necessary to produce a theologian: experience, information, ability. From every possible view-point the Devil is preeminently qualified to formulate a system of doctrinal statements having all the earmarks of genuineness and credentials of authenticity.

In our discussion of the Devil's theology we shall not, at the present, touch upon the theories and vile imaginations of demon-possessed men, but the finer phases of truth, beautifully presented by his apostles with a show of orthodox reasonableness. By the term Devil's theology—doctrines—we do not mean his beliefs—get the distinction—but what he wants us to believe. He is every whit orthodox; he believes the Old Book; he does not indorse the *new theology*, or the so-called higher learning, only as it may be turned to his advantage. The Word of God is a mighty reality to him; he has met its blazing truths, and has been burned by its power. He has millions of skeptics and doubters blindly following his delusions, but he is a believer in the " old school "; he " believes and trembles."

We call attention to the term " doctrines "—therefore religious beliefs: reasonable, plausible, satisfying beliefs. What are they? First:

Ritualism is Religion; when we have gone through a certain proscribed programme—whether it be a chant, reading prayers, or burning a dim light—there you are. How do we know we are religious? We have gone the rounds, said the required number of Ave Maries, counted the rosary, etc., etc., therefore the work is done. It sounds harsh to place these beautiful ceremonies, which have doubtless comforted so many hearts, in the enemy's catalogue; but the Pharisees were rigid ritualists, yet Christ denounced them as miserable hypocrites—" whited sepulchres." Anything he can get us to adopt, having a semblance of reality, yet does not save—does not deal directly with the sin question, he shouts over our delusion. He appropriates Ritualism for Religion and it becomes his doctrine.

A second doctrine: Good Resolution for Regeneration. There has never been as much strenuous evangelism, of a certain quality, as we arc having to-day. Great cities unite in stupendous revival effort; no expense is spared; the leading masters of assemblies are called as workers. The zeal and motives of it all are commendable; but the bane of such evangelism is this: the work stops at the resolution period. Men are brought under conviction, and the Devil at once proposes his compromise. Not until the " big meeting " closes do the convicted multitudes discover the deception. Herein is the explanation of the lethargy, depression, and utter indifference which so often obtain after a " sweeping revival." Faith is then shaken, and sometimes permanently, in the truth of a conscious, know-so salvation. If the Prodigal Son had stopped after passing a good resolution with himself he would have died at the swine pen without the knowledge of the father's love, the kiss, the robe, the ring, and the fatted calf. A sinner must not only " quit his meanness " but straighten out his meanness. Regeneration is not by the will of the flesh, the will of man, not of blood; but it is to be born of God—born from above—a new creature. Doctrines floating under the banner of evangelism which do not get believers into the kingdom must be listed with the enemy.

A third doctrine: Sentiment is Salvation. We are a sentimental people; esthetic and humanitarian developments of recent years have done much to soften our barbarian instincts. If sentiment were salvation, this land would be redeemed. Many think we are rapidly becoming a saved nation; those who enjoy such reflections should stand at the entrance of any theatre on Sunday, or a pleasure garden, or a ball park; then hurry around to the entrance of the finest, best equipped church in the city for comparison. Sentiment is educated emotion. Rome used to shout over the bloody scenes in the amphitheatre; now we can weep over the unfortunate girl who goes down in spectacular glory behind the footlights. Sentiment makes us rejoice with those who do rejoice, and weep with those who weep; it moves us to deeds of charity. Satan then has no difficulty in persuading us that we are religious—spiritually redeemed; if we weep over our loved ones, our emotions are very religious. The most grief we ever witnessed at a funeral was in the home of a saloon-keeper; the dead wife and mother, a depraved opium and morphine eater; the home was utterly irreligious, but the grief was hysterical, explosive. The sacrifices of God are a broken and a contrite heart—over sins committed, producing a godly sorrow, and not a sentiment.

Again, the Devil takes great delight in telling the unsaved and unchurched masses that religion is all selfishness; the poor are made to feel that the Church is the rich man's institution. Notwithstanding the efforts of God's people to reach and help the lost they are represented as mean and selfish, pretending a pious fraud, with no bread for the hungry and no helping hand for the needy. We build stately temples of worship to gratify our pride and vanity with money earned by the sweat and toil of the poor man; money that ought to be given to the poor. Judas protested against breaking the alabaster box. The church is a place for dress parade; the humble and meanly clad are not wanted. All such is malicious slander against God, His Church and His people; but as stereotyped as this may sound, it is being used effectually everywhere. If a church preaches salvation from sin, it is the poor man's best friend; but reference to the church and the preacher is often hissed in gatherings of toiling men. Unless there shall come to this land the establishment of the righteousness of Christ, as taught in His Gospel, we shall see another reign of terror; the fires of restlessness, hate, and discontent are smouldering in every shop, factory, and mine. " The Golden Age will never come until it is brought in by the Golden Rule of Christ." The Devil is busy keeping these facts from becoming known. The doctrine stated: we are in it to serve a selfish end; take away our hope of advantages, and our faith becomes religious junk.

CHAPTER 16. THE DEVIL A THEOLOGIAN(CONTINUED)

One of the Devil's tactics is to make much ado about nothing. It is astonishing how sane people can be deluded over childish non-essentials. Think of the doctrine of Abstinence; at certain seasons be holy with a vengeance. It is a mortal sin to let down during certain days and moons; no meats, no riotous gormandizing, no wine, no dancing, no theatre going, when the season is holy. But are we not so commanded concerning the Sabbath day? The Sabbath day must be kept holy, but if our moral standard and relationship fall below during the week what we are supposed to make them on Sabbath, our piety is a farce.

An incident will illustrate. It was a steamboat excursion; drinking and dancing were freely indulged in by the hilarious passengers. A *parsoii* was among them; he danced not, neither did he look upon the wine that was red. He looked sad—*it was Lent.* One week later we beheld this same *parson* in full evening dress gracefully waltzing with one of the lambs of his flock. Amazing spectacle! Robes of holiness to-day, with fastings and prayers; to-morrow, broadcloth, perfume, patent leathers, and arms encircling a maiden in the dizzy whirl of the dance.

Paul saw such times coming and warned against them.

There are many more, but we shall mention only one more: the gigantic system of saints' worship. What does this mean? Anything that diverts and absorbs the attention away from things fundamental is surely of evil origin. His fall began when he conceived hatred and jealousy of Jesus; now if he can get people to pay a part or all of their homage to Mary, or any one of the many " saints," just so the Son of God is robbed of His glory and neglected, his devilish malice is somewhat gratified. There is a long list of dead worthies who are reverenced and supplicated unto daily; but high over all is the " Virgin Mother of God." After the birth of the Saviour Mary was the wife of Joseph, and bore children as a natural mother—she was not a virgin. " Thou shalt have no other gods before me; " " Thou shalt not make unto thee any graven images—thou shalt not bow down to them." " Doctrines of Devils."

Spiritual minded students of the Bible and human conduct are forced to the conclusion that the Devil is not only a wise theologian, but he is a great *preacher;* and, as we have learned, he has a mighty gospel which he preaches with effectiveness and power. He has clearly defined doctrines which he promulgates at such times and places as will best meet the desired end. But with cunning craftiness he preaches his dogmas and tenets everywhere: housetops, society parlours, centres of business, legislatures, court rooms, barrooms, and bawdy houses, as well as in pulpits. This sounds like a strange mixture: " the sacred desk " associated with such an array of evil—*ad absardum.* If the pulpit is immune, why Paul's exhortation? Doctrines presuppose a preacher, and also an effort to gain an audience whenever and wherever possible.

Yes, the Devil preaches, and if doors are barred he forces an entrance: home and foreign missions, slums, emigrants, aristocrats and sports. He has access to scores of avenues where the Gospel of Christ never enters; but under the cover of human interests he takes the field with our Lord Jesus and His ministers, offering a more beautiful, excellent, easier and successful way. As God's method of saving the world is by the foolishness of preaching, what better agency of opposition could be launched than *preaching?* Nothing. Far stronger is the expulsive than the opposing power. The most dangerous poison in the world is the kind that hides its death in a cup of sweetness; a child eats a sugar-coated pill and never recovers. Hell is peopled by the multitudes who have drunk at the Devil's fountain of soothing, satisfying poison. He keeps his deluded patrons from the fountain of cleansing by an easier way to delectable fountains, the waters of which paralyze with the chill of death.

We note another very remarkable fact concerning the Devil's doctrines and his style of preaching. Christ's ministers often fail because of a lack of adaptability; " he overshot his crowd " is the comment often heard. The genius of this subject does not make this mistake; he is a past-master at adaptability; to those who have a feeble, fluttering conscience for spiritual things he has the sincere milk of the word that soothes and sustains; but for his robust followers, whom he has bound in chains stronger than those which bound Prometheus, he gives the meat of diabolism, prepared and seasoned by a skill of six thousand years' practice.

Place your ear at the keyhole where his children are conducting a "revival meeting"—high carnival of sin—and hear the ideas of God, salvation, preachers, the Church, and the hereafter. This is the strong gospel referred to; the gospel that fires the masses with hate and prejudice against the only means of human redemption. Yes, he preaches, preaches, preaches, and from every nook and corner; ten messengers to one preaching the Christ; his preachers support themselves, and touch the highways and byways; his lines are gone out into all the earth, circumscribing sea and land. The Devil gets an intelligent hearing. He has a long catalogue of doctrines, but he does not believe a single one of them. We should be wise enough to eliminate them from our creed also.

CHAPTER 17. THE DEVIL'S RIGHTEOUSNESS

"Woeuntothem!forthe   yhav eg oneinthew ayofCain."—. *Jude ii.*
"For they being ignorant of God's righteousness, and going about to establish their own righteousness, have not submitted themselves unto the righteousness of God."—*Romans x. 3.*

We are becoming, according to the canons of this world, a righteous nation; the standard of civic and commercial righteousness is elevated as never before. Sleuth-hounds are scenting every indication of misrule and running to earth evil-doers, high and low. Our cities are keeping tab rigidly on sewerage, cesspools, and outhouses; a persistent war is being waged o* flies, mosquitoes, and germs of all kinds. Private citizens are everywhere organizing to cooperate with officials for public welfare. Corporation and municipal rings must answer at the bar of an outraged public conscience.

Righteousness is in the air; it resounds from the pulpit, platform and press. Chautauqua specialists who have discovered some deflection in the political and social woof and warp declare, amid salutes of fluttering handkerchiefs, the righteousness of twentieth century standards. Preaching on the cardinal doctrines of the Bible has been displaced by rhetorical messages on altruism: light, ethics, mercy, cleanness, goodness. " The fatherhood of God and the brotherhood of man" with a flavour of intellectualism, is the gospel that is now being emphasized with much gusto, and never fails to solicit the indorsement of all denominations. " Be good and do good " is the *multum in parvo*of pr esent day righteousness.

Who but a chronic faultfinder could object to this upward move, so obvious now in all directions? The world is getting kinder, more sympathetic, more charitable; creed lines are dissolving like snow under an April sun; sectarian prejudice is dying under the withering frown of new ideals. Does this not indicate a gradual leavening of the "whole lump "? The spirit of Christ, they tell us, is being adopted everywhere. He is mounting the throne of universal empire, and the time surely is not far distant when the social, political, commercial and domestic life will be regenerated by His influence. Yes—it would appear so to be; much that is done bears a Christian label; it comes in the name of Christ; but, says a writer, " it is the Christ of Bethlehem and not the Christ of the Cross." It is the human Christ and not the sacrificial—the exponent of a blood Atonement.

The righteousness that has the full swing of modern religionists makes much of Christ's " example," His beautiful character and self-abandonment—" He went about doing good." Much attention is given to studying His leadership, His pedagogy, His art of public address, His humanity. His example and not His sacrifice saves the world; step by step the human Christ has displaced the Christ of Calvary; His atonement was misguided zeal. This propaganda, on the surface, '.s reasonable and popular; but close scrutiny will reveal a poison as dangerous as it is subtle. It leaves out the Blood; it is a glorification of Man. " Count the number of the beast, for it is the number of man."

This issue is an old one; it became an entering wedge in the religious life when the first services were held after the Fall. Cain and Abel made altars; Cain piled his high with beautiful, luscious fruits of the field. No festal board ever looked more tempting, loaded with sweet smelling fruit, having variegated colours, than the altar which Cain presented to God. They were the results of his own sweat 'and toil;

he offered them as the " first fruits." But God rejected the offering; somehow the very beauty and attractiveness of it all insulted Him.

Abel's altar was smeared with blood; on top lay a limp, bleeding lamb. Nothing attractive about this picture; our esthetic nature recoils at the gore and cruelty of such an offering. Yet God graciously accepted this bloody, unsightly offering; and no doubt rained fire upon it—anyhow, Abel was justified. Why did God reject the one and accept the other? Cain and Abel alike had been taught from their infancy that " without the shedding of blood there shall be no remission of sin." By transgression man stood as an alien before God; he had forfeited divine favour. Notwithstanding, Cain boldly brought before God a bloodless sacrifice, and presumes to force Him to accept it. Through all the millenniums before Christ every approach to God must contain in the sacrifices and offerings an element which reminded God of the coming Atonement. He dedared: " For the life of the flesh is the blood, and I have given it to you upon the altar to make an atonement for your soul. For it is the blood that maketh an atonement for the soul " (Lev. xvii. 11).

Coming directly to the point: all this new notion of things, touching Man's religion, fast becoming prevalent is the " way of Cain," with a twentieth century touch and terminology. What is the essence of this new righteousness? what does it do? Observe, it sets aside God's estimate of man, and ignores the plan of redemption He established at the beginning in types and shadows, then consummated in the atoning death of His Son on the Cross. The righteousness of to-day has much in it to commend; but it utterly disregards the only feature upon which God places emphasis. The Blood and the Cross, as of old, is an offense; they have found a more excellent way, but it is the " way of Cain." It is offering self-righteousness rather than seeking the righteousness of God. The bloody offering of Abel suggested suffering, punishment, death, judgment—but it honoured God. Modern righteousness scoffs at the Abel offerings by hanging a wreath of flowers on the Cross, bearing a perfumed tag, " With sympathy." It is Cain setting up business in town once more. A sacrificial propitiation for sin is unnecessary when we have " inherent goodness." The modern righteousness contends that each man has self-redemptive qualities; all he needs is a chance. Salvation is not internal, but external.

The Cainites are filling the earth; they are preaching the popular sermons, writing the magazine articles, the poetry, the fiction; they occupy the chief synagogue seats of seminaries; they are conspicuous at all chatauquas and baccalaureate occasions.

It is a well-known psychological fact that evil cannot exist apart from Personality—whether it be bad laws, bad books, bad town, or a bad house. Whence comes all this audacious, undermining insult to the whole sweep of God's plan for saving the world? Whence comes all this preaching about righteousness which places the crown on man, and robs the Cross of its glory? The righteousness being sounded in double diapason and angelus keys is *the righteousness of the Devil*. Bear in mind it is *Righteousness*, and a high type of it, he demands; he wants the offering of Cain to cover up all the needs of the soul—cheat the blood of its merit—insult God, and lead the race through a bowery of flowers, fruits, and music on to its ruin. Anything to cheat the depositum of the Gospel—that which gives a title to heaven—the precious Blood. The righteousness that leaves out the Blood is the " way of Cain "—" the righteousness of the Devil."

CHAPTER 18. THE WORLD'S TEMPTER

" Again, the devil taketh him up into an exceeding high mountain, and showeth him all the kingdoms of the world, and the glory of them; and sayeth unto him, All thesethingswillIgiv ethe e,ifthouwiltfalldo wnandw orshipme ."—*Matthew iv. 8-9.*

Temptation is a seduction: meaning to allure or entice one to evil. It is submitting a proposition which carries with it inducements of pleasure or gain. The mind that accedes readily and willingly to an act is not tempted. A temptation is a clash of wills, one being superior to the other if the contest results in a yielding. The word embodies the idea of an elastic—" stretched to the snapping point." If there is no response, no struggle against desire—it is not a temptation. The Master was very man as well as very God; yet strange as it may seem—*He was really tempted,* and just as we are.

Our purpose in this discussion is not to analyze the different phases of our Lord's temptation—the tests to which He was subjected,—but we wish to emphasize one thing: He was *tempted..* The appeals came from His old time enemy; His rival for supremacy. He was not taken unawares; the facts were clearly before Him, just who and what it all meant—yet He was tempted. The diabolical assault did not cease until His threefold nature was " stretched to the snapping point." It came from an inferior being, and for sake of illustration, had the scheme succeeded, the Sun of righteousness would have gone down forever. Not only would the great plan of human redemption have proved abortive, but Satan would have snatched the sceptre from the hand of the Anointed One and shouted his victory in the face of God. We are amazed to think of the only Begotten being near the yielding point in the presence of the fallen Lucifer, but the Book says He was tempted.

Some may contend that He could not have yielded; all the while He was conscious of divine security. This conclusion forces another untenable proposition: If He could not have yielded, His humanity was not real, but veiled in His divinity; the temptation was only a shadow. We insist that as a man Jesus was tempted; He could have called to His aid supernatural intervention, but He did not. The issue was met as every man must meet it; it was manhood that conquered. Had He yielded, both manhood and divinity would have become subservient to the enemy. " Fall down and worship me " was the proposition.

Now we wish to make a few deductions from our Lord's temptation. Whatever includes the greater includes the lesser—*a fortiori.* Natural man reached his highest expression in Jesus of Nazareth; He was God's exponent of human perfection. There were no weaknesses, no lack of pose or symmetry; His penetration and judgment of others were absolutely accurate. From the beginning He had known the Evil One who faced Him. Now, with all those perfect endowments, the record says *He was tempted.* The ingenuity of Satan was sufficient to bring out all the resources of the Son of God. Here was the greatest, wisest, purest and strongest man that ever walked upon the earth—susceptible, influenced, strained to the " snapping point" when attacked by the Tempter. What will be the inevitable fate of you and me, dear reader, whenever he selects us as his victims?

The unmistakable teachings of the Word are that every temptation to which man is or ever has been subjected came fresh from the seething caldron of the pit. The student of human conduct has observed universal adaptability of all temptation. A great sagacious intelligence seems to be managing personally, through his cohorts, this campaign of promising propositions. There are some who can be incited to commit horrible crimes, such as murder, incendiary, born perhaps with vicious tendencies, but this class is comparatively small; others are susceptible to deeds of milder character. It would matter little to an army approaching a fortification where or how the attack should be made if the walls at every point were weak and crumbling. No time is spent in reconnoitre and playing for position; but if the battlements be strong, a faulty place must be located if there be one. Satan rarely ever blunders in laying his temptations; he is a most skillful strategist. As the world's tempter he reveals an ingenuity that is truly astounding; it should cause the bravest heart to shudder once the eyes are opened to the source. Knowledge of his approaches, marches, countermarches, advancings, and retreats—all with a specific object—ought to be a great breakwater.

A writer gives us a striking word picture of Satan's methods: " As the enemy who lays siege to a city finds out the weakest portion of the wall, or the best spot to batter it, or the lowest and safest place to scale it, or where the intervening obstacle may be easiest overcome, or where an advantage may be taken, or where an entrance may be effected, or when is the best time, or what is the best means to secure the desired end, so the arch-deceiver and destroyer of souls goes about, watchful, intent upon ruin, scanning all the powers of the mind, inspecting all the avenues to the heart and assailing every unguarded spot. Sometimes he attacks our understanding by injecting erroneous doctrine; sometimes our affections by excessive devotion to things we love; sometimes our wills by strengthening them in wrong directions; sometimes our imaginations by vain, foolish, trifling thoughts; and sometimes our feelings by too high or too low excitation."

Some one has called Satan and his subordinates not omnipresent, but " shifting imps." They swarm the air, invisible, because they are spirit, watching for opportunities to edge their way into the hearts of mankind. They are shifting position, always to a point of least resistance. Like a current of electricity, always flowing from a point of higher potential pressure to one of lower, if points are connected by a conductor. The metallic substances from which the current starts and towards which it flows are called " electrodes," and are always of different potentiality. The current passes from the one of higher to the lower. Man in his own strength is the lower, and unprotected by the Spirit of God cannot resist the evil currents flowing from Satan continually.

CHAPTER 19. The Confidence Man

" In whom the god of this world hath blinded the minds of them which believe not, lest the light of the glorious gospel of Christ, who is the image of God, should shineuntothem ."—*2 Corinthians iv. 4.*

History is one long, tragic recital of human sorrow and suffering; but there is far more unwritten history than has ever been recorded on the printed page. Along the march of civilization all that has come down to us are the lives and doings of great men; we know little of the heart agonies of the race—such as cannot be recorded—language is inadequate. Most of history is a record of man's inhumanity to man, but historians deal with these dark pages only on the higher levels. The greatest suffering, the bitterest cries of anguish, the deepest wails of despair are in the lowlands of human life: down where its pathos can never be known. The darkest tragedies of war are lost by the gallant heroism of some officer; the blood and carnage are overshadowed and forgotten by the heralds of victory. The real pathos of war remains unnoticed by the chroniclers and correspondents; it is found in the heart suffering of the dying in the trenches; the black pall that settles over the homes made desolate by the news from the front.

The saddest stories of life will never be told; they are the voiceless agonies and smothered sobs from victims of human treachery and deceit. Millions are shambling on their weary way, waiting for the end, whose hearts are dead and buried in graves of misplaced confidence. More domestic lights have been extinguished, more love dreams turned from a sweet phantasy to an horrid nightmare, more bodies fished from the river, more shocking tragedies have resulted directly from this cause—misplaced and wrecked confidence—than from all other causes of human wretchedness.

An illustration from actual life will serve to bring the caption of this chapter—the Confidence Man— out in bold relief. An honest old farmer, whose horizon had not extended beyond the obscure Indiana neighbourhood, sold his little home and started for Kansas, hoping to enlarge his possessions and give his sons and daughters a larger sphere of opportunity. That they might see the wonders of a great city, arrangements were secured for a three days' stop-over at St. Louis. The Confidence Man saw them pass through the iron gate into the lobby. He first noted the train on which they had come to the city. With great enthusiasm he greeted the old gentleman, introduced himself, extending a business card of his " firm." With cunning palaver, and the guilelessness of the farmer—item after item of information as to name and where they came from were obtained. The man who said he thought he recognized the old gentleman soon became satisfied of it— having an uncle living in the same county— and " I have often heard him speak of you, etc., etc."

It required only a short time to not only gain the confidence of the whole family, but also to get all the facts concerning their business affairs: how much the little farm brought, and how much they had left to begin life in the west, and actual cash on hand. There was not a hitch in the scheme; the new friend (?) loaded them with kindnesses and courtesies, paid all the bills at lunch and theatre— took the young people into the mysteries of the great wonderland— all so new and strange.

It was the last afternoon; father and Mr. Confidence Man were returning from a tour of sightseeing. They met a man walking in great haste; looking up he saw the two men, and suddenly laid violent hands on the " farmer's friend," demanding the payment of a note three days overdue. They quarrelled; all manner of apologies were made, that he was " entertaining an old friend, etc.," all of which caused the Shylock to grow more enraged and unreasonable; they almost came to blows.

Finally the old man's benefactor asked to see him for a moment alone. Then meekly humble, and with many regrets, asked for a loan of enough to pay the note. " We will go right down to my office, and I will reimburse you with big interest for the kindness." The honest old man was only too glad for an opportunity of returning, by such a little act, the kindness that had been shown him. The note was almost one thousand dollars; when the bills were counted out, less than ten dollars remained in his purse—the savings of a lifetime.

Proceeding on their way until they reached the first saloon, " It is my treat, uncle," said the man.

After the drinks were served, he asked to be excused for a moment, and stepped into a back room from the bar—he was seen no more. After a long time, the barkeeper informed the old man that his *friend* was one of the worst crooks in St. Louis. With less than ten dollars he staggered out of the saloon, wandered over the city dazed and half insane. On the following day he was found down on the wharf crying like a child. What had happened? He had been in the hands of a Confidence Man.

There are being formed in all walks of life—high and low—associations and alliances, spurred on and incited by extravagant promises—the hook baited according to the fish—which culminates in certain disaster. The pathway of life is strewn with victims of Confidence friends—instead of friends. As in all these subtle and dangerous diversions we believe every trap and scheme are under the direct control and supervision of Satan—playing the role of Confidence Man. Many with a natural impulse for pleasure knock, and at once arms are wide open to receive them; lust beckons, and the Broad Way becomes choked with her votaries; covetousness shouts her promises, and the love of money soon burns out every high and holy aspiration. Fame holds the chaplet in full view, and men are ready to exchange heaven in order to have it pressed upon their brow.

But alas, in the end—in the end—" it biteth like a serpent and stingeth like an adder." When the curtain falls, too late to recover, we shall be found on eternity's shore, shipwrecked, robbed, ruined—victims of the great seducer. No one but an incarnate devil could stoop to the low plane of Confidence Man in business and social life; but think of what it means: by flattering promises, smiles, and kindness force an entrance into the heart life, and when once in possession, desecrate, prostitute, and destroy. We insist that it takes a devil-possessed man to operate in this particular field, and the world is full of such. We therefore conclude he is the god of this planet, blinding the eyes of his unnumbered victims.

CHAPTER 20. THE TRAPPER

"And that they may recover themselves out of the snare of the devil, who are taken captiveb yhimathiswill   ."—*2 Timothy ii. 26.*

"Surelyhewilldeliv erthe efr omthesnar eofthefo wler."— *Psalm xci. 3.*

To be a trapper requires something more than setting traps and baiting them. The old trapper returns from a season spent among mountains, rivers, and forests—ladened with valuable furs of every kind: beaver, bear, otter, fox, mink, wildcat, coon, opossum, etc. Remember the animal kingdom is infinite in variety; no two alike. A trap that will catch a beaver will not answer as a bear trap; a coon and a mink are as far removed from each other as a polished American and a native of Madagascar. A coon will not go within a rod of a chain, but have little if any keenness of scent for protection. A rat will not go near an object if the smell of human hands is on it.

Volumes of natural history would be inadequate to give the details of differentiation of the animal kingdom. The old trapper in his log cabin has never read a page of zoology, but is far more familiar with the ways of the furry folk than the scientists who write our books on natural history. The trapper is a graduate from the school of Association; he has studied the traits and pranks of the forest inhabitants by observation at close range. He knows just where the mink can be caught, and just how the trap must be baited and concealed: he has the same information about all the rest, and can apply it. Once when a child, we were enraptured until late bedtime by the stories of an old trapper: telling about " the different varmints." Without drawing on his imagination, he could have added many chapters to the tales of " Uncle Remus." The facts about our furry friends are far more interesting than fiction; the trapper knows about these facts.

The Psalmist calls Satan a fowler; one who sets traps for old and young as the fowler sets traps for fowls. How is it done? Leaves and weeds are carefully cleared away, and the trap is skillfully set by a trigger, so that the slightest touch will spring it. The ground is also cleared for several rods leading off in front of the trap; suitable food is scattered under the trap and all along the clean strip of ground. The birds excitedly follow the line of " food "—walking under the trap where it is scattered in abundance. In the scuffle, the trigger is soon touched; behold the trap falls, and they are caught; oh, how they beat their heads against the prison bars until they are covered with blood, but all is over. They are caught in the snare of the fowler.

Every animal and fowl will flee from the approach of danger; the trap must be hid, or in some way made to appear as something harmless; nature has endowed them to seek always self-preservation. With nothing but instinct to guide, they are easily caught by the skill and cunning of man, but never caught in the open; some, however, are more easily caught than others, but they must be trapped.

The Bible teaches that the Devil is a trapper; hib snares are set everywhere—they are man traps; no spider ever spun a web more accurately for the moth than Satan's traps to catch men. It requires certain bait and certain traps for each particular animal and bird, but the snares for men are legion. Man has a threefold nature: body, mind, and spirit; each of these have many avenues of approach. As the trapper gains his knowledge of the furry tribe by association, so the Trapper of men, by the application of supernatural powers, in close contact and intimate association through the past millenniums, has become intimately acquainted with man.

There are no facts touching his habitat, food, passions, ambitions, weaknesses, yearnings, etc.— whether in the realm of body, mind or spirit—but the cunning trapper of the pit is more minutely acquainted than man is acquainted with himself.

If guileless and unsuspecting men and women were the only victims, the situation would not be so serious; not that one soul is of more value than another, but the facts are: *no one* seems to be capable of discovering his hidden snares. The greatest and wisest—Alexanders, Anthonys, Napoleons, kings, sages and philosophers—have been captured by him at his will. What a shudder would go over the race if it could penetrate the veil of mystery and see the traps towards which we are moving; moving on to certain capture, but for Providential oversight and guidance. Domestic traps, political traps, social traps, business traps, religious traps; the location and bait are suited to individual likes and dislikes.

"My soul be on thy guard; ten thousand foes arise."

Our country is just beginning to awake to a system of trapping now being carried on in every city and town, so gigantic and heinous that we are dazed and frightened at its boldness. The great White Slave Traffic is carried on by traps, pure and simple; as carefully planned and skillfully executed as the methods of an old trapper who remains in the primeval forest to supply the fur market. The feelers and tentacles of this human devil-fish are running out in the highways and hedges: the factories, mills, department stores. But the traffic is not confined to the poor, uneducated girls at the ribbon counter or waist factory; girls of culture and experience are caught, but the bait used is very different. When once caught, not one in ten thousand ever escapes.

A being less than a fallen archangel could never have instituted the White Slave Traffic. A man or woman not incarnated by the Devil or some of his minions could never promulgate a system so vile, so inhuman, so hellish, as the traffic of innocent flesh and blood, to be offered and burned on the altars of lust for gain. Compared with the White Slave Traffic, as it is prosecuted by the panderers and procurers, negro slavery, at its worst, the extermination of which the bloodiest war ever fought on this planet was waged, is like the vilest ribaldry ever sung in a den of vice to a Te Deum. Lest we forget—Satan is an expert trapper—the king of trappers.

Chapter 21. The Incomparable Archer

" Wherefore take unto you the whole armour of God. . . . Stand therefore, having your loins girt about with truth, and having on the breastplate of righteousness. . . . Above all, taking the shield of faith, wherewith ye shall be able to quench all the fierydartsofthewick   ed."—*Ephesians vi. ij, 14, 16.*

When traps, tricks, seductions, and quackery, temptations, etc., fail, Satan adds victims to his long list by destroying them at long range. While in a mountain peak vision of inspiration Paul sees the enemy as a wrestler, a trickster, a schemer, and even a more dangerous role than either: a skilled marksman. By keeping close to God, and keeping ourselves unspotted from the world, we may stay his blighting touch from personal contact; but there seems to be no absolute safety until we are shielded by the " whole armour of God."

There are " evil days," days of visitation and distress, over which no one has control; at such times we may not be conscious of any satanic presence; yet confusion, doubt, fear and anxiety have complete control over mind and heart. These days, and their depressing effect, can only be warded off by the protection of the " whole armour "; for emphasis, Paul mentions it twice in the same paragraph. An armour is a coat of mail covering the body, made so as to be impenetrable to the missile of death. The Apostle does not stop with a partial equipment; the head and feet also must be properly covered. Especially does he emphasize the *shield*—that great polished, concave steel disk, strapped to the left arm, so that a thrust from sword, arrow, or spear can be easily deflected. As it is carried on the arm it can be raised or lowered so as to protect the whole body.

This arrow-protecting shield must be wrought in faith, that mysterious relation which unites the soul with God. The antithesis of Paul's language implies that when Satan makes certain efforts to wound the soul, the shield of faith alone can save. The fight is not ended when we come out victor in a hand to hand conflict, but must next prepare to meet a shower of " fiery darts." A dart is an arrow shot from a bow; a fiery dart is a flaming torch attached to the arrow.

In all ages, until the days of powder and firearms, soldiers were equipped with bow and arrows. Arrowheads were made of steel, and as keen as needles. The battle-axe and broadsword were used when the lines met, but showers of arrows would fall upon the enemy with as much fatality as a round of grape and canister. Often the arrows would be freshly dipped in a deadly poison, and in that case the slightest wound would result in certain death. When a fort or city was being besieged, the arrows would carry a ball of tow, having been saturated in oil; hundreds of these flaming darts would fall on the inside of the fortification and start a general conflagration.

This method was practiced by the American Indians when they could not reach a fort, blockhouse, or stockade because of the white man's gun; these flaming torches, falling in great number, were more to be dreaded than the tomahawk and scalping knife of the savages.

Satan shoots " fiery darts "—arrows—at us; he may come, as he did to the Master, and find nothing in us; our hearts may be clean. But from a source entirely unexpected—here comes a flaming arrow— burning its way into the heart, igniting with hatred and misunderstanding friends and enemies in a manner never dreamed of before. How often the blow comes from the one place least expected, and for that reason all the more deadly.

We are guarded in some directions, but over the walls of our stockade the Devil sends his fiery darts, and we are swept away in a satanic conflagration.

It requires the " whole armour "—and the shield of faith to quench the flaming arrows from his quiver. He is the world's incomparable archer; when all other methods fail, he shoots us with poisoned, fiery darts.

The mother of Achilles baptized him in the river Styx, making him invulnerable to the weapons of the enemy; she held him by the heel during the baptismal ceremony; the heel only remained untouched by the protecting waters of the fabulous Styx. One of the gods became acquainted with this fact, and shot him to death in the heel, the one vulnerable spot.'

Again, we repeat, we are not safe without the " whole armour of God," and the " shield of faith." Bear in mind, also, the Incomparable Archer takes a more deliberate aim if it is a shining mark, and exults most when he can lay low in the dust, wounded and disabled, one dowered with unusual capacity for noble service.

CHAPTER22.T heF atherOfLiar s

" Ye are of your father the devil, and the lusts of your father ye will do. He was a murderer from the beginning, and abode not in the truth, because there is no truth in him. When he speaketh a lie, he speaketh of his own: for he is a liar, and the fatherofit." —*John viii. 44. .4*

"Sinhasmanyto ols,butalieisahandlewhichfitsthemall." —   *O. W. Holmes.*

Satan opened his propaganda with a slanderous lie; this lie was believed by the innocent parents of the race. Simple and modest as this lie seemed to be, it opened a crevice in the moral government of God. Confidence, fellowship, and filial relations were destroyed by the breach. The nature and character of a lie may best be understood, and we can get the estimate God places on it, by carefully studying the damages it wrought. Eden was lost, God's favour lost, peace and plenty lost, innocence lost; humiliation, fear, banishment, toil, sweat, suffering and death took the place of Eden's pristine glories.

Nothing so reveals the depths to which Lucifer had fallen—and his great intelligence, losing none of its acumen, exercised in a way fitting to his depravity of character, as the launching of a lie. He has done nothing since—which more clearly exemplifies the Being our Bible teaches that he is. An egg was laid and a lie was hatched; this lie has gone out spreading at a geometrical progression until the infinitude of God's footstool has felt the discordant jar.

A lie, and the Father of it; think of this tremendous statement. The thought will overwhelm our intelligence. Suppose all' the peoples that have lived on the earth were lined up: to simplify matters—consider the billion and a half supposed to be living on the earth to-day; just a small part of the number belongs to civilized, christianized nations. What is the situation? Under all the light of education and moral standards, justice, full and untrammelled, can scarcely be had, because of false swearing. An eminent authority says nine-tenths of the race has a price; this means that only one-tenth will rigidly adhere to the whole truth. How few will swear to their own hurt and change not.

Let us study this gigantic proposition from another view-point: every unregenerated heart is full of deceit In every unregenerated heart there is a germ of all the sins of the Decalogue; lying is one of the " shall nots." A close student of men will agree with the Apostle Paul, when he said: " I have no confidence in the flesh." Carnality will not swear against its own interests; the status of civilization, whether in religion or morals, does not seem to control this matter. When we consider the falsehood and false swearing which obtain among the *best* people, socially, financially, and so often religiously, then think of the millions living without moral standards, we can begin to appreciate the amount of lying carried on in this world.

As lying is one of the outputs of carnality, and human selfishness is the tap root of carnality, and selfishness dominates the entire race, with rare exceptions here and there, we can understand how easily and naturally prevarication and lying become efficient tools to further personal interests. We once attended a celebrated criminal case in court; scores of witnesses were summoned on both sides; a bar of attorneys fought desperately every inch of ground. The prosecution covered the case beyond any question to the perfect satisfaction of the jury. And the witnesses were, in the main, both respectable and intelligent.

But behold, when the defense produced their side of the case, the witnesses equally honest looking and intelligent, every point of evidence made by the prosecution was absolutely refuted. A new story was told; a new case from the one just stated. Think of it—on both sides there were eye-witnesses; then every witness on one side or the other perjured themselves—and perhaps all of them on both sides.

So completely has the father of liars woven the spirit of falsehood into the moral fibre of men that a sense of its fearful character is almost obliterated. Men make fortunes, secure positions, are elected to office, destroy rivals, win unsuspecting love, seduce innocence, and subdue kingdoms, by being an obedient offspring of their father, inheriting his disposition and ability to breathe out falsehood. Liars are children of the Devil.

Think of the almost infinite resources for evil: " father of liars " does not fully justify the situation. While it is true he originated the first lie, and the lying spirit has ever widened through the stream of racial propagation; but the clearer interpretation signifies that he is the father of *lies.* " See," he whispers, " the advantages to be gained— don't be white livered—tell it; get the hush money—make the promise—swear you did not see it—tell her how devotedly you love her, etc." Who has not met these insidious pulls on the conscience?

Yes, but he is only acting now as a tempter. Quite true; but when the will gives away, the oath, the promise, the false statement is made under a furious lashing of the conscience. The lie belongs to him; he originated—suggested—formulated it; then literally drew it out with quite as much pain as is felt during the extraction of a tooth by a dentist.

It has been said: " The Devil will leave his own brat on your door-step, then accuse you of being its lather." This is an inelegant, though a striking statement of a great truth. When he is unable to bring forth—deliver, etc.—his own conception, he at once charges us of being guilty of the thing conceived: the lie, vile imagination, or whatever it may be, quoting Scripture to prove it: " As a man thinketh in his heart, so is he." " Now," he declares, " you are guilty anyhow; why not enjoy the benefits?" Father of lies; millions of them spawned every day and hour: big lies, little lies, business lies, social lies, political lies, and not a few—religious lies, black lies, white lies, church lies.

Chapter 23. King ship Of Sa tan

" Wherein in time past ye walked according to the prince of the power of the air, thespiritthatno ww orkethinthechildr enofdisob edience."—*Ephesians ii. 2.*

" For we wrestle not against flesh and blood, but against principalities, against powers, against the rulers of the darkness of this world, against spiritual wickednessinhighplaces ."—*Ephesians vi. 12.*

In a former chapter we discussed the origin of Satan, he being an archangel—Lucifer—a great shining leader of the heavenly hosts; now in his fallen estate he is no less a leader. A writer has said: "He seems to have been the rightful prince of this earth, but he has become the traitor-prince through being untrue to the trust; and the usurper-prince through seeking to retain control of the earth as his own dominion, through deceiving man, to whom the earth's dominion was given, into obeying him, and in utter defiance of God." The angels which kept not their first estate, but went down with his insurrection, are his subjects.

He is superior in all villainies, but the Scriptures call him a King ruling his cohorts, and is the " angel of the bottomless pit." As angel he retains his old title, but as *king,* his relations stand out significantly. As chief Devil—archdemon—the title would imply rather *Primus htter pares;* as commander-in-chief, a general of the highest rank. He is all these things: he gives special oversight to field operations, conducts personally great campaigns, retreats here, advances there, charges yonder—but his real aim is to get this world back under his own control; he would put himself in God's place— drive Him out, dethrone Him, kill Him off, that he might take it all to himself, and rule supremely.

However, he is *king,* and as such he is raised above the rank of leadership and commander. We are already familiar with his rank, but the purpose of this chapter is to show, specifically, that as a king his kingship has a much wider range than the bottomless pit. It is threefold. First, as angel of the bottomless pit, he is king of the *underworld*, the land of shadows, gloom, utter darkness; the land of eternal despair. We must depend upon the *Infernos*, evolved from a burning imagination, in order to get any conception of that region. Fearful as the scenes are, a close reading of the Scriptures will reveal a condition of things so terrible that the things seen by Dante and Virgil are not overdrawn. Over this land of woe and suffering Satan is the unlimited monarch.

Second, he is king of the *upper world.* This statement sounds very strange; it would appear that God is entirely ruled out of His creation. But observe the language: " prince of the power of the air." Just what this means in its fullness no one should dare to be dogmatic, but certainly the language cannot be meaningless words. We can but conclude that Satan, in some measure, controls the forces of the physical world: storms, cyclones, cloud bursts, tidal waves, lightning bolts, earthquakes, etc. Certainly, as a *destroyer*, he uses the agencies of destruction; his business is to fill the world with doubt, fear, distress and suffering.

A man has a little child killed by lightning, and he curses God. Does this not look as if a diabolical schemer was manipulating the affair some way? We must admit his power is permitted, and that proposition forces another to the front. Why does God allow or permit his ravages? We have no answer; the ravages go on. We might ask with just as much reason: "Why doesn't God kill the Devil? " He certainly is able to do it, or at least stop his progress. But He does not; Satan is evidently running at large, filling the world with broken hearts and all the accompanying evils which, otherwise, would not occur.

That we may be able to strengthen our opinion as to the prerogatives of this " prince of the power of the air," let us remember the circumstances of Job's calamities. This case is undoubtedly authentic, and the record says that Satan actually controlled the powers of the air. The servant of Job thought God rained fire on the sheep and burned them, but the whole affair had been turned over to the tormentor. The visitations sent on the faithful man of Uz were not from the hand of God; they were manipulated by his satanic lordship —the Devil. Then a great wind came—possibly a tornado or cyclone— and blew the house down wherein Job's children v/ere enjoying themselves.

Concerning Satan's relation—controlling and directing the forces of nature—we shall not conture a dogmatic position. The definite statements and incidents from the inspired record are significant indeed. Strange things occur: a great vessel loaded with Sunday revellers goes down with scarcely a moment's warning; a tidal wave destroys thousands; an earthquake leaves a city in ruins with fearful loss of life. Does the loving, compassionate Father send these calamities? Would it not be a terrible indictment? But the Bible gives incidents where He did send death-dealing visitations upon the people. Certainly. Many believe that God uses Satan, in his vicious administration, to visit His wrath upon places and people. However, God has given him the title of " prince of the power of the air "— the"wick edness in high places."

The third realm of his kingship is terrestrial; in this he is given a stronger title than prince or king; " The god of this world." Besides, he is the " prince of darkness," and the " prince of this world." So real are his presence and power manifested here that Paul declares the contest is like a wrestling boute. This figure, examined closely, will open up a great continent of truth concerning our enemy, of whom we must meet in hand to hand conflict. See the wrestlers writhe and strain; agony is depicted on their faces; the muscles contract into hard knots, perspiration bursting from every pore. All the strength of every nerve and muscle, wrought up to their full capacity, is exerted. " We wrestle," he declares, and not with flesh and blood; but " against principalities and against powers," " rulers of the darkness of this world."

The great religious reformers since Paul's day have left a similar testimony concerning this terrestrial enemy; his personality has never been questioned by men who were positive powers in the realm of spiritual warfare. After Martin Luther had produced a nation-wide reformation, having been delivered from the bondage of a Benedictine monk by a revelation to his own soul that the "just shall live by faith," he declared: " Satan semper mehi dixit falsum dogma." Shall we deny the oft told story that Luther threw his inkstand at them (demons) when they actually appeared unto him in person? Is it unreasonable? They were alarmed at his triumphs, and wanted to terrify him. The kingship of Satan in the under world and upper world are Bible statements; his kingship in the world about us is a Bible fact confirmed by human testimony.

Chapter 24. The Devil's Handmaiden

"Be not drunk on wine wherein is excess, but be ye filled with the Spirit."—*Ephesians v. 18.*

"Nodr unkardshallinherittheking domofGo d."—*i Corinthiansvi. 10.*

The fallen Lucifer knew from the beginning that his work must necessarily be in competition with the Son of God; therefore he has invested his genius to originate a duplicate for all that Christ has done for us. Knowing that the letter killeth, but the spirit maketh alive, he seeks to furnish all the appearances, and as far as possible duplicate experiences: Reformation without repentance; conviction without conversion; conversion without regeneration; membership without adoption; baptism with water without the baptism of the Holy Ghost; physical and emotional pleasure without the " joy of salvation."

The prophet Isaiah exhorts the people to say: " Praise the Lord," and, " with joy draw water out of the wells of salvation," and, " Cry out and shout, thou inhabitant of Zion, etc." The Psalmist, also, gives out a continuous stream of joyous praise. In all ages people have at sundry times and places shouted out the joy of the Lord. This emotional expression is by no means the only test of experimental salvation, as nothing honours God so much as simple, unemotional faith; but there are times of refreshing from the presence of the Lord. This contrast of emotional experience we wish to examine.

We must keep in mind the bitter rivalry between the Prince of light, and the Prince of darkness. The heart of a contest of this character is the expulsive power of the one over against the other. Satan studies assiduously every experience, every angle of advancement of

Christ's kingdom, and proceeds to furnish a duplicate. He knows that the followers of Jesus often rejoice with a fullness of joy—unspeakable, as it were; to meet this, he soon discovered that the exhilaration of drunkenness produced a splendid expulsive power. He proposes and promises his followers all the joys furnished by his rival; however pleasant they are always shams, and " at last it biteth like a serpent and stingeth like an adder."

A beverage that would produce drunkenness has been a curse from the earliest history. We call attention to two events, each one of which was so great that it left a blight sufficient to turn the course of human history into darker and bloodier channels. The first followed closely upon the remarkable deliverance from the Flood. The Ark had settled; life began its routine, fresh from the awful calamity. Noah built an altar and worshipped God; but before the perfume of the holy incense evaporated, that faithful servant of the Most High became *beastly drunk*, and his son Ham looked upon his nakedness and shame. The children of Ham must carry the curse until the end. The other followed closely upon a deliverance from fire. Lot was a citizen of Sodom, but he had not defiled himself; the iniquity of the place came up before God, and He destroyed it; not, however, until His angel led this righteous man to a place of safety. Through the entreaties of his designing daughters, as they were resting in the mountains, Lot became intoxicated unto idiocy. We must draw a veil over the shameful scene that occurred during his debauch; but the tribes of Moab and Ammon, warlike savages of the desert unto this day, was the terrible resultant. They are the incorrigible followers of the Crescent rather than the Cross.

Wherever drunkenness has touched humanity it has blighted and withered like a Sirocco from Sahara. No one but a fallen archangel could have invented such a beverage. Yet the character of liquors used by the race in its infancy for carnival pleasures, compared with the output of the modern distillery and brewery, are as moonshine to the blistering heat of the summer sun. Satan profits by experience; he has not been idle during the centuries. Solomon warned against " looking upon the wine when it was red, and turneth itself in the cup"— fermentation. If fermented grape juice should, at that time, bring forth such an inspired warning, what language would be necessary to depict the character of the low grade, adulterated fire-water sold in the saloons and dives of America and Europe?

The true spirit and character of liquor cannot be understood if viewed as a stimulating beverage, satisfying and inflaming human passions. Its Author soon discovered that such an unmixed evil must answer at the bar of an outraged individual and public conscience. He saw that if liquor succeeded in all he had planned, it must send its roots deeper down than taste and appetite. Hence this handmaiden of the Devil has now become one of the most gigantic trusts on earth, blooming out into commercial, political, and industrial proportions. The whole business lives and moves and has its being on misery and bloodshed on one side of the counter; loot and plunder, coupled with an insane lust for gold, on the other side of the counter.

It has not one redeeming feature; but so carefully has it sheltered itself by a devil-fish organization that it stands like a Gibraltar. It has become so great that the actual investments in the business aggregate billions; an army larger than the combined forces, North and South, at any one time during the Civil War are being supported; over one hundred millions go annually into the national exchequer. China has been called a sleeping giant; woe to the nations once she is awakened. In the liquor traffic we have a giant that never sleeps. Twenty-four hours each day—like Giant Despair—he enslaves and imprisons the multitudes. So tremendous has this organization grown that its work does not stop with social demoralization, but with little difficulty can dictate governmental policies, throttle legislation, and bribe juries.

Again, we cannot judge or estimate the liquor traffic until we follow it down through its labyrinth of social, financial, and moral declension. Not until we see it face to face, glaring and defiant, in the haunts where finished products are on exhibition. The " Scarlet Annex," temples of lust, and the White Slaver's headquarters are united in the place where labour troubles are hatched, mob violence gathers fuel, and feud hatred is crystallized into bloodshed. Where gamblers, thugs, yeggmen, murderers, anarchists, jailbirds, and burglars hold high carnival. We must see the bloated faces, the bleeding Magdalenas, human beasts, and wife beaters, as they wallow in filth and obscenity, before the perspective is correct.

The inauguration of liquor as a duplicate for God's greatest manifestation of Himself—the infilling of the Holy Spirit—was a master stroke. In a wild, reckless debauch it supplements man's every need and hunger. In the crazed brain there is a vision of wealth, power, revenge, joy. The drunkard is clay in the liquor-demon's hand; if a coward, liquor makes him bold; if sympathetic, liquor deadens his heart; if honest, liquor makes him a thief; if a loving father or son, liquor makes him a brute. Behold the Handmaiden of the Devil—King Alcohol: the most efficient ally of the " angel of the bottomless pit."

CHAPTER 25. THE ASTUTE AUTHOR

"Till I come give heed to reading."—*i Timothy iv. 1 3.*
"Of the making of books there is no end."—*Ecclesiastes xii 12.*

When we remember the crude methods of book making in the days of Solomon, compared with the facilities of modern publishing houses, his statement has in it a touch of humour. To-day manuscripts are turned over to printers and binders, and in two weeks an edition of from five to fifty thousand copies are ready for the market. There are three million volumes in our libraries; and, a writer has said, enough new books come from the press annually to build a pyramid as large as St. Paul's Cathedral, London. Mr. Carnegie is planting his libraries in every town and city in America.

Evening and morning papers are laid at our doors with flaming head-lines of all that has happened the world over in the last twenty-four hours. Detailed descriptions of murders, scandals, elopements, court scenes, betrayals, etc. Magazines, representing every phase of life and industry, are multiplying continually. The literature of a nation is potentially its food for character building, morally and spiritually.

Now what are we reading? Editors are calling for " stuff" with " human interest." The manuscript with " preaching " gets a return slip instead of a check; writers are governing themselves by this canon. The most popular writers of fiction a decade ago, who wrote books with high moral and spiritual tone, have step by step eliminated *religion,* and now deal with Socialistic questions and New Thought problems.

The most popular novels are teaching false standards of life, and some of the " best sellers " are base libels on religion and the Church.

This is the situation, and a close observation of the output of the high-class, reputable publishers will confirm it. Why is this the status of our book makers? Book writing and publishing, like all other branches of human endeavour, have become commercialized; writers and publishers are pandering to a vitiated taste for revenue only. It is not literature editors are seeking, but stories that will sell.

A librarian of one of our large cities told the writer that seventy-five per cent, of the books called for and read were positively harmful to the highest ideals. If such is true on this plane of literature, what can be said of the publishing houses which produce nothing but books utterly vile and immoral? It is said there are two thousand publishing concerns in New York City issuing just such literature, circulated secretly in many instances. An army of writers are employed to furnish so many " thrillers " monthly. These " stories " deal with the lowest, vilest passions of humanity. What is true of New York is also true of Chicago and other cities.

Enough stories have been written of the James Boys, Wild Bill, Buffalo Bill, and other border heroes (?), could they have lived to take the least part in so many situations, to have required a century to pass through them all. As much blood as was shed actually at Shiloh has been shed by the writers of border outlawry during the past twenty-five years. The indirect influence of the books of the James Boys have caused more bloodshed than those Missouri bandits spilt by their unerring marksmanship.

A penniless orphan boy was adopted by his well-to-do uncle, who gave him all the comforts and opportunities of an actual son. Early in his teens he became a novel fiend—the lowest and vilest type; reading several each week. When scarcely fifteen years old, he armed himself with his uncle's pistol, took from the barn the finest horse, and left in the early morning. The gentleman, suspecting the truth concerning the missing horse and boy, called a neighbour, and the two gave chase to the young ingrate. They came upon him late in the day, and as the uncle seized the bridle rein, the nephew shot him through the heart, and wounded the neighbour before he could be pulled from the horse and overpowered.

A beautiful girl was found dead in Central Park, New York. Her face, form, and the fabric of her clothing showed plainly that she belonged to a home of wealth and culture. In one hand was an empty vial labelled deadly poison; in the other hand, gripped in the paroxysms of her last struggle, was a paperback novel. The explanation was simple: the heroine had a downfall, and rather than face her shame, committed suicide.

If you will observe the throng of factory girls, overworked, underpaid, heart-hungry from which the White Slaver reaps a rich harvest, they will be reading the class of book mentioned. They enter into the sacred relation of married life with false, distorted ideals, the end of which is often ruin: infidelity to marriage vows, abandonment, and divorce court.

There is another department of literature, written with but one purpose in view: the overthrow of orthodox faith. A thousand questions are raised which the common people cannot answer. Why is it the unchurched masses are continually drifting farther and farther from the Church and what it stands for? Labour unions have almost repudiated religion; class hatred was never more pronounced than to-day, notwithstanding the loud proclamation of human brotherhood. Say what you will as to causes, this condition is not an accident; we must go far up the turbid stream to find the source of these defiling waters. When we find the source, it will be found that behind all these insidious influences stands the inspiring Author.

Why is there such an incessant effort to divert the minds of the best people from personal relationship of Jesus through faith in His blood? Where is the author, the editor—even religious editors—who stand four-square for the Bible of our fathers and mothers? We are glad to say there are a few exceptions; but the drift of writers and editors is away from fundamentals. Satan boldly and thievishly appropriates every available avenue to the soul; wherever his cold, clammy hand touches, it leaves a chill of death. Beyond a question more writers than we ever dreamed are only amanuenses of the Astute Author.

CHAPTER 26. The Hypnotist

"Even him, whose coming is after the working of Satan with all power and signs andlyingw onders."—*2 Thessalonians ii. 9.*

"And deceiveth them that dwell on the earth by the means of those miracles which hehadp owertodointhesightoftheb east." —*Revelation xiii 14.*

"Awakethouthatsle epest,andarisefr omthede ad."—*Ephesians v. 14.*

Just where the natural and the supernatural exists is a most difficult psychological problem. Many marvellous doings and strange apparitions, from the beginning, were attributed to the supernatural. These same wonders are now known to be the application of physical and psychological laws. The " enchanters," " soothsayers," " diviners," " magicians," and " fortune tellers " have awed the simple-minded and superstitious in all ages. A clear understanding of Hypnotism, Mesmerism, Telepathy, Odylic Force, Psychological Phenomena, Clairvoyance, Black Art, and Spiritism, will throw light on many of these supposed supernatural mysteries. Under whatever name demonstrations may be known, they are all various phases of certain well-established laws touching our physical, mental, and psychical being.

One of the most common, and best understood, of these mystery workings is Hypnotism which, defined, is " an artificial trance, or an artificially induced state, in which the mind becomes passive." The subject, however, acts readily upon suggestion or direction; and upon regaining normal consciousness, retains little or no recollection of the actions or ideas dominant during this condition. Hypnotism is purely mental and physical; but this strange power which one can exercise over another strikingly illustrates the influence which Satan exercises over millions of blinded subjects. We shall avoid any attempt to discuss the science and philosophy of Hypnotism; this phase of the subject is not germane to our discussion.

All these subtle laws of mind, acting in relation to the body, only now being understood by scholars, are undoubtedly familiar to our common Enemy. We believe that centuries before man knew anything about psychic laws, as understood to-day, strange, unaccountable influences were operating on the wills and consciences of men. Hypnotism is a form of sleep; but during the time the subject can receive and obey instructions. They are absolutely under the control of the hypnotist.

Paul caught an extraordinary vision of sin when he exclaimed to the Ephesians: " Awake thou that sleepest, and arise from the dead." Here is a fearful figure of sin: that it is sleep—semi-consciousness — unconsciousness; yet they think, act, move about, enjoy, love, hate, etc., etc., and they are as one asleep. Observe this state is, if allowed to remain *in articulo mortis*, Hypnotism, conducted by the Master of Black Art; and they obey his will, over against observation, warning, wisdom, experience of others, even of themselves. Voices may call loud and long, but do not awaken the soul under the satanic spell.

There are many freaks of hypnotic influence which illustrate vividly the power of sin—and back of the sin, the sin Personality. We have seen subjects placed under hypnotic sleep, and they would remain in this condition for twenty-four hours. The demonstration was made in a large department store, facing a stone-paved street, which roared day and night with cars and heavy traffic. Hundreds of people swarmed about the sleeping man, laughing and talking loudly. Not until the hypnotist came and touched the subject did he arouse from the heavy slumber.

A still more remarkable demonstration is reported to have been accomplished in an Eastern city. We give as authority the *Associated Press.* After the subject was placed under the hypnotic trance, he was dressed like one being prepared for burial, then put in a coffin, hauled to the cemetery in a hearse. The " corpse " was then lowered in a grave of the proper depth, the grave filled to the ground level. The air tube from the coffin to the top was large enough to enable a light to be reflected on the face of the sleeper. " Buried alive," said the report. He was left in the grave several hours.

If superior mind force can accomplish such marvellous feats on human will, what may we expect from supernatural mind force with a burning ambition to subdue? The columns of our *dailies* are filled with reports of the doings of men and women that cannot be explained on any other hypothesis.

Think of the insane, unreasonable, illogical risk in all manner of sin— for what? A momentary taste of some " forbidden fruit." We hear that self-preservation is the first law of our being; but how often this law is utterly ignored for sensuous gratification. Those who do these things are unable to understand their insane conduct until it is all over. " Oh, I can see it all now," is the despairing cry so often heard. Of course, the hypnotic spell is removed. How easy it is to sit and philosophize on the actions of people. " Why would any sane person do such a thing? " A sane person would not; the why of all these human twists is very simple when we are willing to admit the literal teaching of God's book concerning our indefatigable Enemy. " The apostate angel and his followers by pride and blasphemy against God and malice against men became liars and murderers by tempting men to do sins "(Jude 6, R. V.).

Why did the Prodigal Son do such an insane, sinful act? Why? Well, he came to himself, but not until the harm was wrought. Why have ten thousand prodigals since that day been guilty of the same insane conduct? The answer is obvious. Why did Judas sell his Lord?—He who had been so highly honoured: chosen, ordained, sent out? " Satan entered into Judas; " there you have the whole truth. By and by, Judas came to himself; then remorse and despair not only caused him to return the money, but destroy himself.

In a subsequent chapter we shall discuss more particularly the suicide problem; but we are satisfied Judas was a victim of two Satanic schemes: the hypnotic spell deadened his reason and judgment to do the deed; then, after the Crucifixion, despair gripped him like a vice. Who would say that Judas was excluded from the Saviour's dying prayer: " Father forgive them "? Peter denied Christ, then lied and blasphemed about it. He was restored; but Satan's power over Judas was not broken. His end was Satan's finished work. What he did to Judas he purposes to do with every " subject "—utter destruction.

We once saw a snake charm a bird; the serpent's head was lifted several inches—eyes blazing, and red tongue flashing. The bird fluttered, gave a piteous wail, but was helplessly walking into the jaws of death. Now the question arises: what about the freedom of the will? Do we ever cease to be free agents? Certainly we do not; the hypnotic subject exercises free choice; that is never destroyed, but he acts under a compelling *vis titurga*—power behind.

CHAPTER 27. DEVIL POSSESSION

"As they went out, behold, they brought to him a dumb man possessed with a devil. Andwhenthede vilw ascastout,thedumbsp   ake."—*Matthew ix. 32-33.*

"O generation of vipers, how can ye, being evil, speak good things? "—*Matthew xii. 34.*

One characteristic, which has been prominent in the varied manifestations of Satan studied so far, is adaptability. Methods that were available in the days of our Lord cannot be used successfully now. By some secret unknown to us the Devil enters into the souls of men. This is a mystery; so is, also, the filling of the Holy Spirit a mystery. The Devil possessed King Saul, Judas, Ananias and Sapphira, and many are the instances recorded in the ministry of the Saviour. Devil possession, it seemed, was very common; Christ was continually casting them out, and He also gave His Apostles power likewise to cast them out.

We do not believe the Enemy has abandoned his old profession: an evil spirit despises a disembodied state; if people are fortified and shielded against his entrance—then the swine. As cold air whistles and roars about every crack and cranny, entering in from all directions, so evil spirits—Devil and demons—press their entrance into the soul. If it is true they cannot enter except by permission,—they pry and pound until resistance is impossible, unless divine reinforcement comes to the rescue.

There are maniacs, violent, desperate, incurable, to-day as truly demon possessed as was the man who lived among the tombs. This, however, is not his modern *modus operandi;* desperate maniacs could then terrorize a whole community. Our great asylums have solved this problem; even the immediate family is relieved of the burden and fear. Those who do not accept the theory of demon possession should explain a case at present in one of our institutions. It is a boy, at the time it attracted attention, only twelve years of age, thin, emaciated, and by no means abnormal in any particular. This child would remain quiet for days; during this time he possessed no strength beyond one of his age. At unexpected moments he would be seized with violent contortions, frothing at the mouth, and snapping like a mad dog; and a continuous flow of the most obscene language and blasphemy while the spell lasted. This is not the strangest part: he had the strength of a giant; it required four or five men to overpower him. One man was helpless in his hands; he would literally hurl them to the floor. Compare this story with the one in the fifth chapter of Mark: " And when He was come out of the ship, immediately there met Him out of the tombs a man with an unclean spirit, who had his dwelling among the tombs; and no man could bind him, no not with chains, because that he had been often bound with fetters and chains, and the chains had been plucked asunder by him, and the fetters broken in pieces: neither could any man tame him."

In countries where the gospel light has not yet shown full-orbed, demon possession with manifestations similar to those of Bible times are known to be common. F. B. Meyer relates numerous cases in Russia; many by prayer were cast out in the name of Jesus Christ. " I confess" he says, " these incidents have greatly impressed me. I wonder how far it would'be right to deal with certain forms of drunkenness and impurity as cases of demon-possession. It may be there is more of this demon work among us than we know, and especially in cases of mania." Dr. Howard Taylor, of the China Island Mission, it is said, was accustomed to diagnose the symptoms of demon-possession in the same way as of any other disease. Dr. Nevins, of the Presbyterian Mission Board, tells of hundreds of cases, witnessed by himself, where by faith in the Son of God the demons were cast out, and the victims were clothed and in their right mind.

Cotton Mather says of Salem witchcraft: " Those persons said to be bewitched would swoon, froth at the mouth, their bodies would cramp into irregular shapes; meanwhile they would utter accusations against good people who, they said, had bewitched them. This excited sympathy of the court. As soon as the court rendered judgment, those bewitched victims would be relieved of their physical cramps and mental torture." Salem witchcraft was real cases of demon-possession, but the court blundered in that the demons were located in the wrong persons.

Sir Walter Scott says that similar manifestations of Satan as were witnessed at the time of the Salem witchcraft occurred simultaneously in every country on earth. He writes again: " Anna Cole, living at Hartford, was taken with strange fits which caused her to express strange things unknown to herself, her tongue being guided by a demon. She confessed to the minister that she had been familiar with a devil." Pages could be filled with modern examples which coincide so exactly with New Testament records that we have no doubt the causes are the same.

Professor Webster, late of Wheaton College, said in a lecture before the students: " I once knew a man possessed of a demon. He became so vicious that he had to be confined in a cell in jail. When he heard any one swear or blaspheme, he would go into convulsions of laughter. When any one used the name of God or Christ, he would curse everything good, and foam at the mouth. He possessed superhuman strength, like the man living among the tombs."

The soul is God's masterpiece, created to be the habitat of the Paraclete, but may, as truly, become the habitat of a demon. We believe that Diabolus has so organized his forces that his minions represent various sins; they are specialists—skilled labourers: drink demons, lust demons, lying demons, anger demons, theft demons, pride, blasphemy, etc. Demon possession to-day expresses itself in sins we try to control by means of courts, education, etc. Homes become a miniature hell because of drink, pride, lust, or lying demons.

Our penitentiaries are crowded with men who were controlled by a demon, forced them into drink, anger, or theft, until the deed was committed. We may feel thankful that there are so few Scriptural cases of demon possession about us—the old time possession. The wise Enemy has shifted, but at the same time has greatly enlarged his field of operation. There are no witch victims to-day: the courts would not punish the witches, but the bewitched would be safely cared for in an asylum. But observe, there are ten thousand other insidious ways in which he possesses men and women, enlarging his kingdom daily; his victims multiply, but not among the tombs. The name of Jesus continues to be the only remedy.

CHAPTER 28. DEVIL OPPRESSION

" So went Satan forth from the presence of the Lord, and smote Job with sore boils fromthesoleofhisfo   ottohiscr own."— *Job ii. 7.*

" Who went about doing good, and healing all that were oppressed of the devil."— *Acts x.38.*

A necessary concomitant of demon possession is its influence upon the individual's moral faculties; an entirely new type of moral tastes are developed: tempers, sympathies, and, especially, doctrines which are diametrically opposed to genuine spiritual religion and revelation. Demon possession bitterly and persistently rejects, whether by a nominal professor or unbeliever, the doctrines of repentance, new birth, etc., through a blood atonement.

In demon possession the fight is on the inside; in demon oppression the fight is on the outside. In the one, Satan controls the man: body, mind and soul; in the other, he depresses, afflicts the man: body, mind, and soul. In the one, the victim is the incarnation of evil; in the other the victim is generally the purest and holiest of men and women.

The Devil or demons may be ejected by the power of the Holy Ghost, but the hellish enterprise is never given up; all the engineering of the pit is utilized to keep ransomed souls out of the kingdom. Once a choice is made, all hell is aroused unto wrath and riot to torment, nag, and finally drag the discouraged pilgrim back into sin and apostasy. This is often accomplished successfully through an afflicted body. Who knows but that the drama enacted in the land of Uz has been repeated many, many times since Job sat on his ash pile?

" But," says the objector, " sickness and disease come as a result of exposure, natural laws violated, inoculation by infection and contagion." True, but remember he is the " prince of the power of the air." What he did once he can do again, and more efficiently. Think of the strenuous war being waged on germs, microbes, and bacilli; we have diseases more violent than ever before. Yet when the race of life was less complicated and simple, none of the modern precautions were thought of; flies swarmed about everything placed on the table, and their mission thought to be one of beneficence. There are many actual and implied statements in the Bible which teach that disease and sickness are often the result of demon oppression; a large part of our Lord's ministry was relieving those who were oppressed of the Devil and demons.

Then his work is just as effective in the realm of the mind; the mental faculties, filled with confusion and doubt, are incapable of exercising their normal functions. Multitudes are able, because of their intelligence, to guard the approaches through the physical organism, or to the extent of subjection at least; but are as completely oppressed in mind as others are in body. We do not claim that any are entirely immune from his attacks; but he is wise and sagacious enough to select such victims for specific oppression as will best satisfy and gratify his diabolical pleasure in seeing the followers of his rival suffer. He oppresses only such as he is unable to possess. Many have been so troubled mentally that Christian living becomes a life and death struggle. Here we find another example of " wrestling not with flesh and blood."

But some of Satan's greatest victories and rejoicings come from soul oppression. We believe this to be the real secret of our Lord's agony in the garden; it was the Devil's last opportunity to thwart the great plan of salvation. Oh, to cheat Calvary; put our " Lamb slain from the foundation of the world " in such physical, mental, and soul burdened agony He would refuse at the last moment to do all the will of His Father. How near he came to accomplishing the diabolical scheme we learn from the story as given by inspiration. We remember His piteous remark as they left the Paschal room: " My soul is exceedingly sorrowful, even unto death"; then He cries out in anguish: " If it is possible, let this cup pass from Me." Never was He nearer the great Father heart, and never was He more a man than at this time; and as a man, perhaps during the terrible crisis, He did not analyze His sufferings and emotions. All the powers of hell were combined to crush Him at the hour for which He came into the world.

Every student of soul tragedy can appreciate, in a limited degree, the experiences of Gethsemane. Paul had this exact experience in mind when he wrote of the " evil days " in which we had to "wrestle." What are evil days? Days when the heavens are brass, and the fountains of prayer are dried up; a cold, sinking sensation clutches the heart. The mind is in a jumble, plans are thwarted, the mail brings a message of some deception or betrayal, the hand slips, fires go out, trains missed, pressing duties remain undone; nervous anxiety and evil forebodings chill the soul. The mind and heart are filled with dread; cold perspiration swells into beads upon the brow. Evil days! Oh, how we stumble and blunder; we cannot even think of advancement. Paul says we can only stand still, and having done all, stand. Many who are not familiar with the nature of such " days " will cast away their faith, believing that their " feelings " are the index to the state of grace in the heart.

But, thank God, a crushing defeat came to this traitor-prince in that the full programme leading up to the world's great Atonement was carried out to the letter. It was not the physical fear of death which caused the blood-sweating agony of our Lord; if so, thousands have met the martyr's end far more triumphantly than did He. Some believe it was the weight of the world's sin breaking His heart. Both the physical dread of death and sin burden may have entered into the garden tragedy; but it was, we repeat with emphasis, the myrmidons of hell taking the advantage of His humanity at the crisis of His life: *It was Devil Oppression.*

Devil oppression does not always come in a diseased body, a confused mind, or in days of soul depression. But sometimes they are new, instantaneous, fierce, overwhelming, and always from different angles and approaches. A vile suggestion, a remembered sin, long ago under the blood, a strong inclination to commit revolting deeds. An eminent, and deeply-pious divine of the South tells in his autobiography that while alone in his study, in meditation and prayer, he was strangely assaulted by the Devil. For more than an hour the inclination to blaspheme was almost beyond his control; it seemed that vile oaths would well up in his mouth and almost leap from his tongue. So terrible was the attack that deliverance came only after a long struggle on his face crying out audibly to God. Then the dark cloud of bat-winged vampires, almost visible, left as mysteriously as they came. It was Devil Oppression.

CHAPTER 29. DEVIL ABDUCTION

" Now the Spirit speaketh expressly, that in the latter times some shall depart from thefaith,givinghe edtose ducingspirits."— *i Timothy iv. i.*

" And no marvel; for Satan himself is transformed into an angel of light."—*2 Corinthians xi. 14.*

We used the above Scriptures in a former chapter, but with special reference to " doctrines "; the part we wish to emphasize now, " giving heed to seducing spirits ": that is to say, be led away or abducted by the Devil or demon. There are four classes of people who may be subjected to the seductive influence of evil spirits. We should keep in mind that the " prince of this world " and his emissaries were once angels, and of course, when necessary, can bring their angelic attributes into seductive usefulness.

One of the problems facing the Church and all religious workers is to keep the converts or communicants in line; steady them in the presence of deflecting influences. The Church is suffering from the inroads of every conceivable brand: isms, cults, fads, worldliness, etc., which always mean, not only usefulness paralyzed, but the loss of Church and Bible ideals. How many among us who once ran well, but are now tilted, side-tracked, derailed, and ditched. We are encompassed about with ten thousand plausible, seductive tenets, arguments and theories, which if yielded to will result in utter religious ruin.

There are four classes of possible victims, all sincere and conscientious, none of which are basely wicked. First: the unregenerate who are blindly seeking the light, but following the inner voice and promptings, rather than the Word of God. These become easy victims to the charms (?) of Christian Science, Theosophy, Spiritualism, Mormonism, etc. Once inducted, there follows a mental refreshing, and a carnal peace, which bring the " soul rest " and " assurance " they eagerly sought. These cults are lauded and believed as modern " revelations" but they are only *new clothes* stretched over the dried mental mummies which lived and moved in the early centuries and dead civilizations. Various shades and deductions from old Hindoo philosophy, Egyptian magic, Gnosticism, Stoicism, Estheticism, Asceticism are paraded so as to catch the cultured, twentieth century devotee. In whatever form it may come, the beauty worshippers of Estheticism, the mental anesthetics of Christian Science, or the debasing sensuality of Mormonism, it is " led away by the Devil or a demon."

A writer on modern Spirits says: " Extraordinary spiritism of to-day is but the continuation of the worship of the old idol Tammuz, as worshipped by the corrupt Israelites and Canaanites, and the Adonis, as worshipped by the Greeks. The indecent practices of these mediums made it necessary to seek darkness to cover their vileness." Ezekiel, in the eighth chapter, speaks of it; the Delphic Oracle practiced the same iniquity: the personification of lust.

The second class of possible victims is the regenerated believer or nominal professor of religion. It is the belief of the writer that no greater havoc is being wrought anywhere in the realm of religious aspiration than is being done to-day among professing church-members, sane, perchance—who once knew the secrets of saving faith. To this class there seems to be two horns in the dilemma of abduction. As an eminent author says: " If we give the preponderant attention to the providences which appertain to the body, there is danger of becoming deistical and materialistic in our views. If we study the word alone, without due appreciation of the Spirit and providence, there is danger of drifting away into dead formality, drying up, becoming creedistic, theoretical, and unspiritual."

What can check the materialistic trend of the times? What can save the Church from reflex influences of modern materialism? Somehow, we have reached the place where things must appeal to the senses: we must taste, handle, smell, see, etc.; things in the Church, as well as out, have jostled down to a metallic basis: something for so much. In the same degree, deny it as we will, our religion ceases to be a religion of faith. Then, on the other hand, the history of Christendom from the beginning, without an exception, proves the second horn to the dilemma: as we lose the spiritual afflatus, we become ceremonial. Upon this reef of rocks our Church is crashing to-day. We see only the material; we have a mania for statistics, figures. Our Sunday-schools seek organization, grades, banners, honour rolls, numbers. Great schools are pushed with enthusiasm by unconverted officers and teachers. About ninety per cent, swarm out and away from the Church and rarely if ever remain for the preaching of the Word. In fearful, glaring reality we can see in all this ceremonialism and dress parade Demoniacal Abduction.

The third class is much smaller; they are the select few who live in the inner circle of things. Having been brought from darkness unto light they seek to walk in all the light, and to live continually in the good, acceptable, and perfect will of God. This class are the sworn, uncompromising enemies of Satan's kingdom; but often their zeal is without knowledge. Perchance, many are weak and unlearned. Satan will leave the multitude of mystery workers and formalists to make havoc among these saintly ones. All that he accomplishes here cuts like a two-edged sword: the individual ruin, and the deadening, paralyzing influence to the cause of truth. By what method does he gain access? Abduction is only possible here where preponderant emphasis is placed on the leadership of the Spirit without careful, diligent adhesion to the Word. The Word is the Spirit's weapon;

without it he is handicapped. What is the result? Fanaticism, dreams, visions, wild-fire, extreme positions on dress, food, domestic relations, etc., until they are " led away by a demon beyond recall." Shipwrecked, " affinities," free love, infidelity, are inevitable. Wherever societies, communities, or churches become inoculated with the virus of any of these phases of fanaticism—untold harm surely follows. The Devil is responsible for the religious " craze," and will then exaggerate by lies and misrepresentation before the unbelievers.

The fourth class are, of all, the most to be pitied, and no work of the " angel of the pit " is so hellish as his operation and strategy upon an awakened soul. Those who are in religious work are grieved continually at seeing the process chilled and defeated at a point which would soon result in deliverance from the bondage of evil. Satan actually assumes the person of the Holy Ghost. Strange and amazing as this sounds, it is nevertheless true. As soon as the soul is awakened he assumes a general godfather sort of relation to the penitent one. Advice and suggestions flood his mind: his pride, clothes, reputation, business, and all are used as arguments. " You should be a Christian—join the church—it is your duty; but when you make a start, *be sure* you have a genuine experience. You are conscientious— anything but a hypocrite with you. Now this is not an opportune time, etc., etc.," on and on, until the penitent refuses to arise and go to his Father's house. Procrastination; Satan literally drags him away from the mercy seat.

How can he do this? Where is the Holy Ghost all this time? Why does He not protect His identity? So long as a man is in sin he has a nature that is not subject to the law of God, and cannot be: carnal mind, old man. On this territory Satan has right of way; under the guise of one seeking to help them in their confusion and sorrow, he manipulates until prevenient grace is grieved away. The poor deluded soul has been " led away by a demon." It is Devil Abduction.

Chapter 30. The Rationale Of Suicide

" And he cast down the pieces of silver in the temple, and went and hanged himself."—*Matthew xxvii. 5.*

" He drew out his sword, and would have killed himself, supposing that the prisonershadb eenfle d."—*Acts xvi. 27,*

The Devil was a murderer from the beginning of human history; his first bloodshed was fratricide— growing out of religious jealousy. He is the father of murder and murderers. This crime, provoked or unprovoked, is monstrous; the passions that incite it were born in the pit. Then what may be said of self-murder: suicide? It is the most fearful, unnatural, abnormal of all forms of demise. Every impulse of reason and judgment revolts at the thought. The Master Himself drew back from death; the Book says death is an enemy.

Various and satisfactory explanations always follow the news of suicide, " financial reverses," " ill health" " public exposure" " domestic troubles" " melancholia" etc., etc. These explanations will not stand under the light of close scrutiny; reverses and misfortunes are generally contributing causes, but not sufficient to answer fully the horrors of suicide.

We hesitate to discuss this gruesome subject, but the character study of these pages would not be complete without it. We speak not with any degree of dogmatism or claim of superior insight to hidden truth, but in the fear of God we are persuaded that not a single case of suicide, since the race took up its painful march, came about from natural causes. Satan, the embodiment of monstrosities, is responsible.

Suicide is numbered among our vexing problems; reckoned on the basis of population, suicide has increased one hundred and fifty per cent, in two decades. Scientists are tremendously interested; thoughtful people are alarmed. Psychological and sociological authorities tell us that *poverty, disappointed affection*, and *dissipation* are the chief causes. The problem can never be solved by social and scientific speculation. We must cross over the borderland into the supernatural before all the angles of the problem are met and satisfied.

There is some strange history connected with suicide. Greek philosophers wrote about it; whether among heathen or civilized peoples, it was considered a disgrace. The Greeks buried them at night— on the public highways, and without religious ceremonies; and their goods were confiscated for the Crown.

We wish to emphasize a former statement: suicide is *unnatural;* it sets aside her first law. The law of self-preservation holds good in every walk of life; when we cease to love life, the deepest principle of our being is out of balance. The body is holy, and when it is destroyed, the highest *felo de se* is committed; not only so, it is assuming the prerogative which belongs alone to God. " It is appointed unto man once to die." Life is a sacred gift.

There are two kinds of suicide: the responsible and irresponsible. The first often appears to have been deliberately planned, the act of a sane, rational mind. However, the best alienists say some phase of insanity always accompanies this rash act. The second are mentally deranged, for which there are many causes. Two classes, also, as to character are found among the unfortunates: the religious and irreligious. What then may we conclude from the most mysterious tragedy on earth?

Satan always scores a victory when a neighbourhood is shocked by the news of a suicide; the victory is direct and indirect. If the victim is prepared or unprepared, sane or insane, the crime can somehow never be forgiven. A strange demoralizing influence is always felt; a feeling of horror and depression. If the victim is pious, and many, many are the most devout in the church, do they forfeit their salvation by the *felo de se?* Not necessarily. Now we wish to say here, with every word underscored: *no sane, devout person will destroy themselves.* Where, then, is the motive and victory of Satan? Much, every way. The whole church or community will be religiously paralyzed. It is generally believed that no self-murderer can be saved. But behold a sainted mother in Israel found hanging in the barn: we have in mind just such an incident, and remember also the gloom, the depression, the silent whispers, the downcast look on the faces of all who knew her. Satan may know that he has nothing directly to gain, but, indirectly, doubt and discouragement prevail. Anything to get the world to doubt God.

A very devout man, writing of a personal experience, says: " There seemed to be some designing spirit near me for days that constantly whispered in my ear, and sometimes it seemed almost audible, Go kill thyself; you have disgraced your Redeemer and you are not fit to live." Scores of such testimonies are on record.

Think of the logical traps used by the Designer to incite the deed: if poverty, " My family will be cared for better than I can." If a suffering body, " This will cure me of my pain." If fear of exposure, " That will end it—charity will forgive me then." If hopeless over some sin, " Better die than face the disgrace. It will solve all the problems," says the Tempter. It is often remarked concerning some one: " How cowardly; " but it is not cowardice; it is inability to answer the Devil's logic to commit suicide.

Again, gruesome as it is, and here is more strange evidence in favour of the satanic explanation: It is fearfully contagious. Professor Bailey, of Yale, said that the report of a suicide by any special method will be followed by others in the same manner. Morbid, despondent people hear of it and follow the example. That which should be revolting in the extreme possesses a strange charm. Ingersol toured the country at one time advocating suicide as the best way out of life's difficulties. Many took his advice and a fearful epidemic followed. One young man in a rural community of Illinois committed suicide; three others, all associates, followed in a few weeks. No special motive could be given for either. We are forced to place the blame where it belongs, and sympathize with the victims.

CHAPTER 31. DEVIL WORSHIP

" Then he forsook God which made him, and lightly esteemed the Rock of his salvation. They provoked him to jealousy with strange gods, with abominations provoked they him to anger. They sacrificed unto devils, not to God; to gods whom they kne wnot." —*Deuteronomy xxxii.'15-17.*

" But I say the things which the Gentiles sacrificed, they sacrificed to devils, and not to God: and I would not that ye should have fellowship with devils. Ye cannot drink the cup of the Lord, and the cup of devils: ye cannot be partakers of the Lord's table ,andthetableofde   vils."—*1 Corinthians x. 20-21.*

Satan's consuming passion is thirst for power. He is the " prince of darkness," but also the " god of this world," and this long period of satanic rule is called *night.* God's glorious Sabbath of rest was superseded by the black intervention of toil and suffering. Satan's scheming fight has been for the rulership of this world. He succeeded in winning the entire antediluvian world, which to save the coming generations necessitated the Flood. He began adroitly with the only remaining family; swept the postdiluvian peoples into midnight heathenism. Today, nearly one billion descendants of Noah worship not God—but *demonian*—demons, just what the Greeks and Romans worshipped in Apostolic times. No less than two hundred and fifty million are devil worshippers by name; Satan began his fight of opposition by assuming the form or incarnating himself in the body of a snake. Therefore it is not an accident, growing out of mythological tradition, that serpent worship has been the chief religion^ of many peoples. The Egyptians worshipped Set which personified all evil— . enemy of all good—they called Typhon, a monstrous serpent-like animal. To this god human sacrifices were offered on great religious holidays. It is no accident that the millions who know not the true God nevertheless, some way, learned to worship the Devil, and generally in the form of a serpent. The

Egyptians had a serpent-god in Typhon; the Canaanites worshipped a snake in the days of Abraham; the Babylonians worshipped Python, which is a specie of the most deadly reptile on earth, and another name for Typhon. On the monuments and tablets of many dead civilizations the engravings of serpents show their particular customs of devil worship. The American Indians were snake worshippers; in Ohio an altar more than a half mile in length remains in good preservation. This altar is one of the wonders, being a perfect outline of a gigantic snake. We readily see that tribal association and tradition have had nothing to do with the customs of our own aborigines; the same being who inspired the peoples of the Old Orient, millenniums ago, to worship the snake-devil inspired our red men in his primeval forest.

David speaks of demon worship: "Yea they sacrificed their sons and daughters unto *Shadim*" Jere-boam built places to worship evil spirits; the ordained priests to serve the altars of " Satyrs," and children were offered. The Molech of the Canaanites was also devil worship; when the Israelites forgot God, they "caused their children to pass through the fire unto Molech," an evil god. The damsel whom Paul delivered possessed the spirit of Python—the snake. The priestesses of the Delphic oracles prophesied by the spirit of Python; this was the dominant religion throughout Greece. The Actez war god of the Montezumas, where two hundred and fifty thousand human skulls were found in the temple, was a bloody system of devil worship. The Yezidis of Persia, descendants of the early Python worshippers, worship the Devil to-day, and are known as such.

We are not confined to heathenism, ancient or modern, to find the same religion of " divinations." The best authorities of Spiritualism believe that the supernatural, occult demonstrations, as produced in their seances, are from demon agencies. The whole system of mythology grew out of what is to-day the work of mediums. The Old Testament is filled with statements concerning " familiar spirits "; they heard voices, received messages, saw physical disturbances— just as may be witnessed at any spiritual seance. The most reliable of mediums do not deny that evil spirits (damned demons) come to them at times. One fact is noteworthy: when men and women become spiritists, they discard all the essentials of the Christian faith. They are modern types of demon possession. It is no unusual thing during a seance to hear a regular clash of voices: blasphemy, oaths, vulgar, obscene language, terrible threats, etc.

What connection do we find between Devil worship and modern Spiritualism? First, the moral condition among the spiritists is exactly as it was among the ancient priests and priestesses in the temples of Devil worship; they literally worshipped the Devil in their corrupt, degrading practices. Now, among the votaries of Spiritualism, every iniquity, crime, and indecency known among men and women are daily carried on. Such is the testimony of one of their travelling lecturers. One of their noted mediums when under control delivered this message: " Curse the marriage institution; cursed be the relation of husband and wife; cursed be all who sustain the legal marriage." From what source could we expect such a vile deliverance?

Second, their mediums actually pray to Satan. One of their advocates at the opening of a debate with a Christian minister at San Jose, Cal., prayed in the following language: " O Devil, Prince of Demons in the Christian's Hell; oh, thou Monarch of the bottomless pit; thou King of Scorpions, I beseech thee to hear my prayer. Thou seest the terrible straits in which I am placed, matched in debate with a big gun of Christianity. Remember, O Prince of Brimstone, that when thou stretchest forth thine arm the Christian God cannot stand before thee for a moment. Bless thy servant in his labours for thee; fill his mouth with wisdom; enable him to defend thee from the false charges of thy sulphurous Majesty, so that this audience may know and realize that thou art a prayer hearing and a prayer answering devil ” (abbreviated). Similar prayers are frequently published in the *Banner of Light*, the organ of this cult; prayers formulated in the same language as prayers offered to the God of heaven.

It cannot be doubted that Pagan religion and modern Spiritualism are Devil worship, shifting under various forms and ceremonies in different ages and places. Rev. B. Clough, missionary in Ceylon, says: “ I now state, and I wish it to be heard in every corner of the Christian world, that the devil is regularly, systematically, and ceremoniously worshipped by a large majority of the inhabitants of the Island of Ceylon.” We repeat: his consuming passion is to be worshipped.

Chapter 32. Victory Through The Victor

" This is the victory that overcometh the world, even our faith. Who is he that overcometh the world, but he that believeth that Jesus Christ is the Son of God? "—*i John v. 4-5.*

" Ye are of God, little children, and have overcome them: because greater is he that isiny outhanhethatisinthew   orld."—*1 John iv. 4.*

One of the grave dangers of to-day is that Satan is no longer regarded as a Personality. Even among those whose faith is founded on the word of God, the idea of an orthodox devil smacks of superstition and an exploded hoax from the Dark Ages. " Let us hear the love side of the gospel; away with this devil and hell business—it's too dreadful," they declare. His real existence and personality are ridiculed in many pulpits and lecture platforms. When these ideas become common among the people who think, a wide open field remains for him to work unmolested.

We can also go to the other extreme: that is, to think him a greater being than the Son of God. Those who have followed us through these chapter studies will, we fear, come to some such conclusion. Who can be equal for such a mighty Prince? Now this biography was undertaken that we might have a full, life-sized photo of our Enemy. In this we cannot exaggerate the true status of the case; any less conception of Satan than we have portrayed will put us at a serious disadvantage in the life struggle. He is a real foe, and we must meet him in the open, under cover, and invisibly. Let it be written in black-faced caps, and heavily underscored: Satan is all we can find out about him—plus, with emphasis on the plus. We want to keep in mind clearly the Enemy, the battle-ground, and the battle; we can never match swords with him; to ignore him—big, cunning, supernatural, eternally at it—will be the most dangerous folly.

But—there is victory, complete, overwhelming victory for every one who fights; but bear in mind it must be a fighter. There is one Name which never fails to reverberate from the Throne of God to the cavernous pits of darkness; this Name shakes loose the grip, untangles the web of all the allied powers of the Prince of Night. Satan is mighty, Jesus is almighty; he met his Waterloo. Jesus was never defeated. His first defeat was when he was an archangel; he was overthrown and cast out of heaven. Jesus said: " I was present when Satan fell like lightning from heaven." He was also defeated in the wilderness; again in the Garden, and at Calvary. In fact, on every battle-field where he met the Lord Christ the defeat was stunning, humiliating. Now we are in mortal combat with him, and we must not forget—he has been many times defeated. A writer says: " We have the advantage of fighting a defeated foe" Standing alone, we are doomed to utter defeat, capture, ruin; but if our fight is coupled with the Name of Jesus, our triumph is as certain as our defeat will be without Him.

So long as we muster in as munitions of war our intellect, self-sufficiency, egotism, etc., the cohorts will laugh at our delusion. There is but One who can out-general his maneuvres, silence his thunderings, checkmate his diabolical acumen, know his oily, snaky approaches, penetrate his angelic beneficence, understand his insidious schemes: that One knew him from the beginning, and—outranked him in heaven and conquered him on earth.

This question arises: If Satan has been conquered, and Jesus is yet contending with him for world wide supremacy why the almost universal triumph of evil? Why is true righteousness at such a discount? Why are the fighters failing and falling all around us? If these questions cannot be answered with a degree of sound reasoning, the whole problem of life, Bible, God, Atonement, Gospel are in a hopeless tangle. A Chinese puzzle does not compare with a riddle of everything worth while, visible and invisible.

Satan undoubtedly controls the machinery of this world. Then wherein is the " victory that over-cometh the world "? Let us keep in mind the power, resources, opportunities, organization, and management of Satan; also the blindness and bondage of sin, and—the Free Agency of Man. So long as man remains carnally-minded and free, the Enemy has undisputed right of way; while the heart is carnal, impure, unsanctified, the controlling motive power of man's life " is not subject to the law of God, neither indeed can be." He has in his own bosom a traitor, an alien to the government of God. **"T o be carnally minded is death," says Paul. The " old leaven must be purged out "; we must " put off the old man (carnal mind) and his deeds, and put on the new man, etc." This putting off is absolutely necessary.

Jesus cannot only defeat Satan, but He can destroy the " works of the devil "—one of which is the alien principle of our nature. " For this purpose the Son of God was manifested, that He might destroy the works of the Devil." The life, death, and resurrection of Jesus—the God-Man—is an everlasting Atonement and a propitiation for sin. Sin is the Rubicon of our battle; once we solve, in all its fullness, the problem of sin, we rob Satan of his fulcrum power. He came to Jesus and found nothing: no availability, no sin, no yielding, no fellowship. He was tempted, but *without sin.*

Our victory must be twofold: first, through the merits of the Everlasting Blood Covenant we may be saved from sin unto salvation—reconciliation, forgiveness. Then by the fuller benefits of the Atonement we may " enter into the holiest by the Blood." Only the pure in heart can stand the approaches of Satan by way of our natural appetites. The triumphs of modern surgery are only possible by means of sterilized instruments. Please observe—with all the meaning that can be couched in language: the sinful, unregenerated heart is not only in danger of being overcome, but is already in blind bondage to Satan. The power of sin, both actual and original, must be broken by the pardoning grace of God through faith in the Atoning Blood; and the heart cleansed and empowered by the Baptism of the Holy Ghost.

The second inevitable concomitant of victory is copartnership with Jesus, the Captain of our salvation —"looking unto Jesus the author and finisher of our faith." Diabolus and his minions cannot stand before this Name. His final overthrow was when Jesus cried out on the Cross: " It is finished." Now at the sight of Jesus, the Cross, or the Blood, the phalanx of darkness slinks away. Let us lay hold of eternal life by an unfaltering faith in the Blood that cleanseth, and " The Name high over all: in earth, in heaven, in hell." " And they overcame him through the blood of the Lamb, and the word of their testimony." Amen and Amen.

Chapter 33. The Arrest And Imprisonment

" For the devil is come down unto you, having great wrath, because he knoweth thathehathbutashorttime   ."—*Revelation xii. 12.*

" And I saw an angel come down from heaven, having the key of the bottomless pit and a great chain in his hand. And he laid hold on the dragon, that old serpent, which is the Devil, and Satan, and bound him a thousand years, and cast him into theb ottomlesspit,andshuthimup   ,andsetase   alup onhim ."—*Revelation xx. 1-3.*

The fact of a possible victory through the Name of our great Conqueror does not alone satisfy all the items of the indictment. If such were the only background to the picture, great as it is, the human drama is not only a fierce tragedy, but a miserable farce. Thank God, personal victory is not all; there is a rift in the dark satanic cloud which has hung over the world for so many millenniums. Satan is in great wrath, and his power and influence grow steadily stronger; more and more his iron grip fastens about the throat of the world. The Apostasy of which Christ and His Apostles wrote is becoming a reality.

Satan will score one more gigantic victory; then is our "blessed hope of His glorious appearing" when He shall come and catch away His Bride—the Church, both dead and alive; that part of His following who are united to Him and are earnestly yearning for His coming. This event is called by devout scholars "The Rapture." Just where, how, when, or how long, we have only a vague prophetic conjecture. " Where, Lord? " they ask. "And He said unto them, Wheresoever the body is, thither will the eagles be gathered together."

When the Rapture shall have taken place, Satan will have undisputed dominion; then shall the " Man of Sin " appear, setting himself up as

God— to be worshipped. His reign will be the Great Tribulation; all the influences of righteousness will, for the j:ime, be removed—the earth will reek in corruption and bloodshed. It is implied that, so terrible will be this -time, divine intervention must necessarily shorten the Tribulation, else no flesh will be left on the earth. The Great Tribulation will be the climax of the Devil's rule on earth. It seems that he will incarnate himself in a Man, giving him supernatural knowledge and power.

However, something spectacular and sensational will soon occur. When the leader of a gang of thugs or desperadoes is arrested, his followers are filled with fear and consternation; then think of the excitement. An Angel officer will break in on the scene—yes, that is exactly what the Book tells us: the High Sheriff of Heaven will suddenly step down from headquarters, and will lay hold—arrest the Old Dragon—Satan—Devil—Serpent (observe all his names are mentioned). Whatever his titles and distinctions of the past have been, they will not save him in that hour. The Apocalyptic Vision is unmistakable.

Some can see in this wonderful language only an allegory: the good influences are to gradually bind the influences of evil, and to expect such an event as the literal arrest of the Devil is a wild, irrational, unscientific, unreasonable dream. Our Lord said, speaking of the time of the end, that the same social conditions as prevailed in the days of Noah were to be repeated: wicked ones waxing worse and worse; scarcely any living in the fear of God. To expect to see a gradual regeneration of society, politics, commerce, and the Church —until evil will be overruled, chained as it were—seems to be a gigantic travesty on language and the teaching of the Bible.

We prefer to stand by the Book rather than human interpretation—fixed up to justify the methods and results of modern religious propaganda: An angel appears—evidently an archangel: one belonging to the rank of which the fallen Prince formerly belonged. This Sheriff of the skies is equipped for his undertaking; Officers carry handcuffs with which to bind prisoners—the angel has a great chain in his hand; he lays hold—arrests the old skulking, hateful, murderous Devil. This angel-officer has also a key, and it is the key which locks the door of the bottomless pit. This door has been wide open; Satan and his emissaries could go and come at pleasure. Just as an officer arrests a desperado and leads him off to prison—so will the archangel arrest the Devil and lock him up in the pit of darkness and despair. What will be done with his millions of cohorts? We can judge only by inference. We want to stay close to the inspired record; of one thing, however, we are confident: the footstool of God will be absolutely cleared of Devil and demons; " that they shall deceive the nations no more."

The prophetic picture of the divine court proceedings is very specific: we have the exact length of the prison sentence—*one thousand years*. When we remember the crimes, unnumbered crimes, the sentence seems to be an example of court leniency. But this is only a " binding over," as it were, to the real trial and judgment yet to come. This will be temporary imprisonment; but oh, it will be such a glad, happy day. The vision of Isaiah, thirty-fifth chapter, will be literally fulfilled. The sceptre so long in the hand of a traitor—usurper—will pass into the hand of the Prince of Peace. Yes, we will strengthen our weak hands and confirm our feeble knees—Satan at last locked up. We shall witness with joy unspeakable and full of glory—" the Restoration of All Things." " And the earth shall be filled with the knowledge of the glory of the Lord, as the waters cover the sea." Thank God forever.

———————————————————————

CHAPTER 34. THE FINAL CONSUMMATION

" And the devil that deceived them was cast into the lake of fire and brimstone, where the beast and the false prophet are, and shall be tormented day and night foreverande ver."—*Revelation xx. 10.*

After the long term of imprisonment shall have ended, we are told that Satan shall be loosed out of his prison for a season. This is difficult to explain; but we do not presume to question the administration of God's government: " Will not the Judge of all the earth do right? " Satan, like many other confirmed, apostate criminals, immediately on being released, plunges more deeply into crime than before. The long term of imprisonment and punishment hardens and, if possible, more nearly consumes him with wrath.

At once he launches another world-wide campaign of deception, gathering, rallying, mustering, and drilling his forces: those who by an exercise of free choice, notwithstanding the glorious millennium reign, actually fall away and enlist under the black pirate flag once more. He encompasses the whole face of the earth; like a deposed crown prince, he leads an aggressive warfare to regain the honours and influence which he so long enjoyed on the earth.

Now if the binding of Satan is only a figure of the leavening power of righteousness overpowering the evil—what is the *thing* which shall be unchained and loosened? Such a contention is as unanswerable as it is untenable. We will repeat once more, with each word underscored: *Good or Evil cannot exist except in a Personality.* The same school of theologians who deny the personality of Satan, many of them, see nothing in the Person of Christ except a *Christ spirit,* inherent good, etc.; all of which is unadulterated infidelity. Just another method of " blasting at the Rock of Ages."

Satan shall be locked in a prison for one thousand years—then he shall be loosed, and every moment of his freedom will be occupied in preparation for the last Armageddon. He does not foresee future events, and it is possible he does not understand this to be his final struggle; otherwise he would be unable to inspire such a following. As we read this brief but vivid picture of the Gog and Magog engagement, the marshalling and shifting for position of Napoleon and Wellington, preparatory to their decisive battle, in comparison to this gathering, will be like a cadet sham engagement. It seems that the lines of fortification will reach out over the entire earth, mobilizing around the Holy City. The saints, also, are gathered into encampment; whether for preparation to meet the forces of Satan, or for protection, the prophecy does not state; but all the powers of light and darkness are brought face to face.

The battle never reaches a real encounter; the impudence and rebellion of the deposed prince and exconvict arouses the wrath of God as never before.

The cup of His indignation is full to the overflowing, and He brings the fearful conflict to a spectacular ending. The destruction of Sodom and Gomorrah was a microscopic event compared with the rain of fire that shall fall in consuming vengeance upon the Devil and his followers, both men and demons. The saints shall be delivered in that awful hour, and this is the last shifting of the scene; the bell will ring, as it were, and the curtain will fall, closing out the long tragic history of the old world.

We are not dogmatic as to the chronological order of these mighty events, but as closely as we can gather them from the Word, the next move of these wonders in heaven and in earth will be the ushering in of the Last Judgment. The *Deis Ira*br eaks in upon the universe; the Great White Throne will swing into view. During the vision of millennial vision, its reign—John saw " thrones "; Christ and His Church ruling jointly the kingdoms of earth; He then is the Chief Shepherd, the King of kings and Lord of lords—holding the sceptre of universal empire. But now when the *Deis Ira* dawns, there will be just One Throne, and God Himself will sit upon it.

If the reader wishes a detailed description of this Last Day, it can be found in the sixth chapter of Revelation, where the whole programme is thrown into a composite picture: " The Opening of the Seven Seals." Each seal is a separate prophecy or act of events from Alpha to Omega of things. Language breaks all bounds of rhetoric, poetry, and definition: " And I beheld when he had opened the sixth seal, and lo, there was a great earthquake, and the sun became as black as the sackcloth of hair, and the moon became as blood, and the stars of the heaven fell unto the earth, even as a fig tree casteth her untimely figs, when she is shaken of a mighty wind. And the heaven departed as a scroll when it is rolled together; and every mountain and island were moved out of their places."

Note the effect this marvellous demonstration will have upon the followers of the traitor-prince: " And the kings of the earth, and the great men, and the rich men, and the chief captains, and the mighty men, and every bondman, and every free man, hid themselves in the dens and in the rocks of the mountains; and said to the rocks and the mountains, fall on us, and hide us from the face of Him that sitteth on the throne, and from the wrath of the Lamb: for the great day of His wrath has come; and who shall be able to stand."

All the souls that have lived on the earth, good and bad, saints and sinners, Devil and demons, will stand before the Throne and be judged. The words, thoughts, and deeds of men and devils shall be made known. The final doom of the Devil and his angels will be shown up in detail before an assembled universe: the Godhead, angels, archangels, cherubim and seraphim, and all that have lived upon this planet. Hence, the last and final scene of the Epilogue: " And the devil that deceived them was cast into the lake of fire and brimstone . . . and shall be tormented day and night forever and ever." Amen and Amen.

CHAPTER 35. SATANIC SYMBOL IN NATURE

"For the invisible things of him from the creation of the world are clearly seen, beingunder stoodb ythethingsthatar emade ." *—Romans i. 20.*

The evolution of Christian scholarship, during the recent decades, has wrought wonders in bringing about absolute harmony of science and religion. Under the microscope, and through the telescope, men whose hearts are trained as well as their brains, the great book of Nature is found to be a commentator and expositor of the Book of Revelation. They have not only studied and theorized about the science of religion; but by laws of induction and deduction have discovered a " Religion of Science," and when properly understood and applied is not out of harmony with the most orthodox faith.

Just as chemistry, geology, zoology, botany, astronomy, etc., whether seen in the protozoa or the highest type of man; the animalculi (creatures which propagate their specie by millions in a day) or the elephant; the electrons or Polarius (our North Star which is one hundred times brighter, larger, and hotter than the sun)—all demonstrate laws, systems, design, purpose, and beneficence from the hand of a wise Father-Creator: so also are there other things in the physical world discovered by the student of nature which suggest an opposite being.

We remember that even the ground was cursed when sin entered with its defiling touch; where flowers and fruits did once abound has come forth a crop of vile weeds, thorns, and poisonous vines. These occupy and will conquer in any soil on the earth—the Poe or Mississippi valleys, without the diligent, unceasing, systematic toil of man. There must be a continuous fight against these omnipresent enemies—in garden, in vineyard, on farm. Clean out every weed, allow none to produce seed of its kind; then leave the land for one year untouched, and it will be a ragged wilderness. Fruits, grains, and vegetables left to fight with these enemies of the soil, and, without a single exception anywhere, they are soon choked out and will die. Unaided by the skill of the gardener, the end is inevitable.

But, observe again, fighting the soil demons and conquering them is only half the battle. There is not a tree, plant, shrub, vegetable, fruit, nor flower, in any latitude or zone, but that must contend with pests, parasites, and insects of all kinds. The herbivorous enemies are not limited to insects and creeping things, but actual diseases. Several of the choicest fruits have cancer; various blights have destroyed whole crops of cereals. Trees and vegetables have diseases that must be diagnosed and doctored as carefully as the family physician treats pneumonia or typhoid fevers.

But this is not all: whole orchards are killed by the caterpillar; the boll-weevil has been known to devastate great sections in the wheat belt. The grub kills the corn as soon as it sprouts; the potato bug, the tobacco worm, the army worm, the Gypsy moth, celery worm, California scale, etc., on and on, until we find that every fruit, grain or vegetable is beset by some vermin destroyer which, if not removed or poisoned, will sting to death, or gnaw at the vitals until they wither and die. The horticultural kingdom must contend with imps of death until garnered safely in the harvest.

When we examine the animal kingdom we find the same conditions obtain; every animal from the bug to the buzzard, from the ant to the elephant, from mice to monkeys, have a bitter struggle for existence. A distinguished German professor has this to say, addressing the

Fishery Association of Berlin: " War is the watchword of the whole of organic nature; there is a constant war of all organisms against outward unfavourable circumstances, and there is a constant war among the different individuals. The seed grain which falls into the ground, the worm crawling on the earth, the butterfly hovering over the flower, the eagle soaring high among the clouds—all have their enemies; outward enemies threatening their existence, and enemies eating their life and strength." Following these remarks he gave a long list of fish parasites sufficient to destroy the whole finny kingdom.

Another eminent naturalist, speaking of the perils of insect life, said: " With such savage murderers prowling among the shadows, life among our singing meadows is anything but a round of pleasure. The warfare is broadcast. Not even the fluttering butterfly is safe, but is pounced upon in mid-air, its wings torn off in mockery, and is then lugged off to some dark hole in the ground. And the bee returning to its hive is waylaid on the wing, and its body is torn open for the sake of the morsel of a honey-bag within."

Still another scientist tells us: " The microscope shows that these murderous imps appear to have been made to inflict the most excruciating torture upon their victims." He makes special mention of the sand hornet: " He is the greatest villain that flies, and is built for a professional murderer. He carries two keen scimitars, besides a deadly poisoned poniard, and is armed throughout with a coat of mail. He lives a life of tyranny and feeds on blood."

Every drop of water is swarming with hideous creatures which, if sufficiently magnified, would be frightful beyond description; the air we breathe is surcharged with death: infecting organisms which, if the system in the slightest degree becomes unable to eliminate them, bring on dreadful diseases. We must fight for our physical life daily. But for the immunity provisions of Providence, our bodies may be a charnal house, at any moment, of billions of bacilli hastening our end. These are stern facts which face every student of biology or natural history.

As a professor has well said, " He, therefore, who objects to the teaching of the sacred Scriptures concerning Satan and demons, and appeals to the Caesar of the natural world, can get no help, for that Caesar echoes back with thunder tones that there are myriads of living, malignant and destructive organisms in every realm of nature, so far as is known, or so far as one can reason from analogy, that, like Satan and demons, trouble and torment the innocent as well as the guilty; that in some instances these malignant organisms appear to inflict suffering for the sheer delight of doing it"

What is the conclusion of the whole matter: The existence of Diabolus and demonia is a fact of Revelation verified by both science and philosophy.

Table des matières